MODERN COLOR

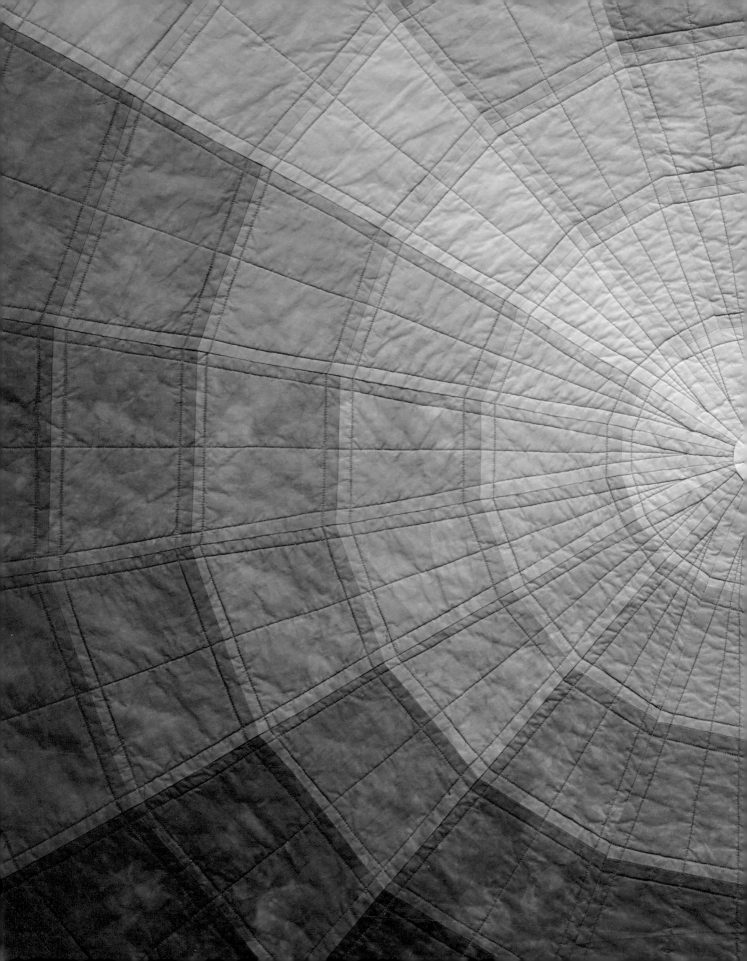

MODERN COLOR

An Illustrated Guide to Dyeing Fabric for Modern Quilts

Kim Eichler-Messmer

stashBOOKS®

an imprint of C&T Publishing

Publisher: Amy Marson

Creative Director: Gailen Runge

Art Director/Book Designer: Kristy Zacharias

Editor: Lynn Koolish

Technical Editors: Susan Nelsen and Carolyn Aune

Production Coordinators: Zinnia Heinzmann and Rue Flaherty

Production Editors: Alice Mace Nakanishi and Katie Van Amburg

Illustrator: Tim Manibusan

Photo Assistant: Mary Peyton Peppo

Styled Quilt Project Photography by Tea Ho, Cover and all other Styled Photography by Nissa Brehmer of C&T Publishing, Inc., Flat Quilt Photography by Diane Pedersen of C&T Publishing, Inc., unless otherwise noted

Published by Stash Books, an imprint of C&T Publishing, Inc., P.O. Box 1456, Lafayette, CA 94549

Library of Congress Cataloging-in-Publication Data

Eichler-Messmer, Kim Lauren, 1979-

 Modern color, an illustrated guide to dyeing fabric for modern quilts / Kim Eichler-Messmer.

  pages cm

 ISBN 978-1-60705-692-8 (soft cover)

1. Dyes and dyeing, Domestic. 2. Quilts. I. Title. II. Title: Modern color.

TT853.E36 2013

746.46--dc23

2013009777

Printed in China

10 9 8 7 6 5 4 3 2 1

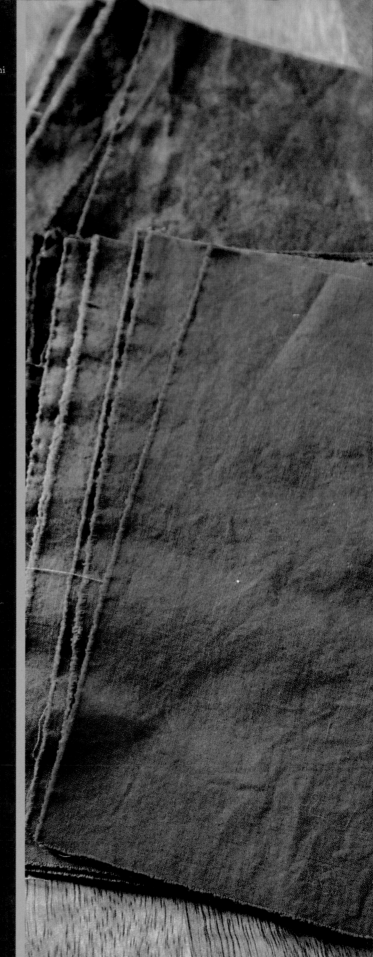

DEDICATION AND ACKNOWLEDGMENTS

I would like to thank my amazing, supportive husband, Simon, who kept me fed and sane throughout the process of working on this book. I would also like to thank my wonderful parents. My dad taught me to sew, and to generally be handy, and demanded a high level of craftsmanship in everything. My mom fostered in me a love of art and knew I was an artist long before I did.

PREFACE

I have been dyeing my own fabric for more than ten years and have been teaching others how to dye fabric for the past seven years. The methods in this book are straightforward and written specifically with quilters in mind. They have even been tested by members of the Kansas City Modern Quilt Guild! The ability to dye your own fabric will allow you to greatly expand your fabric stash and make your quilts more unique. My goal is to lead you on an in-depth exploration of fabric dyeing so that you can gain confidence in the process and ultimately apply these techniques as you make your own unique quilts.

CONTENTS

INTRODUCTION

The Benefits of Dyeing Your Own Fabric

When I first started sewing, I felt completely overwhelmed selecting fabrics for each project. I would go to the fabric store with a specific vision but then find myself changing my mind endlessly and spending countless hours in the store figuring out what to buy. Usually what I desired didn't exist, and I would struggle in my attempt to put together an approximation of what I wanted. Eventually I would leave the store, disheartened, with either way too much fabric or none at all.

When I learned how to dye my own fabric, something in my brain clicked. For me, controlling every element of the quilt is liberating. I can make any color I want, including any value (lightness or darkness) or gradation, allowing for an unlimited palette. I can make any quantity that I need and can always make more of each color if I run out. The uneven nature of hand-dyed fabric adds a unique depth to a quilt. I love that no matter how careful I am, the color never comes out exactly the same from dye bath to dye bath.

This could be frustrating for some, but these variations mark the loving hand of the maker and create a truly individual quilt.

Dyeing your own fabric requires a greater time investment than buying solids or prints, simply because you can't just run out and buy whatever you need. I order my dye and fabric online, so it takes some planning ahead and waiting for shipping. Additionally, it takes time to dye fabric and wash it out before you can use it. However, I find the process of dyeing fabric to be fun, exciting, and totally worth the effort, and I hope that you will, too.

Each quilt pattern in the book gives instructions for the amount of fabric you need to dye. There will be the option to dye fabric for the quilt top alone, or to dye enough for the top and back. Some of the quilt backs in this book are pieced, and some are solid. Feel free to design your own back and use your favorite prints if that seems more appealing. In that case, you will dye only enough fabric for the quilt top.

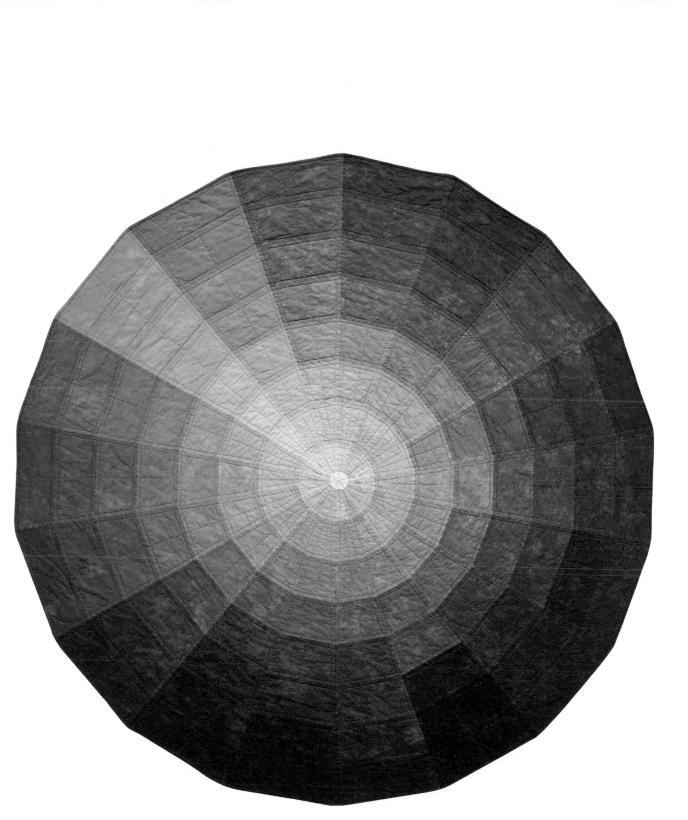

Color Wheel Quilt, 82˝ diameter
2012

LET'S START DYEING

DYES

All the dyeing in this book is done with Procion MX dyes. These dyes are made specifically for cellulose (plant origin) fibers such as cotton, linen, hemp, bamboo, rayon, and Tencel. MX dyes also work on silk, but the color will vary with different materials. Fiber-reactive dyes form a chemical bond with the fibers and have excellent washfastness and good lightfastness. This means that after the initial washing-out process, the dye will not fade with subsequent washings. Hand-dyed fabrics, just like all other fabrics, should be kept out of direct sunlight, which will cause them to fade over time.

Pure yellow dye from Dharma Trading Company, Jacquard Products, and Pro Chemical & Dye

Many places sell Procion MX dyes, and each company gives the colors its own names. These companies also create their own custom dye mixtures. Dharma Trading Company, Pro Chemical & Dye, and Jacquard Products are the three largest dye suppliers in the United States, and each sells many different color mixtures. Rather than using proprietary mixes, I prefer to use only pure hue dyes when possible. Pure hue dyes are those that are made up of only one dye color rather than a mix of colors. I do this for several reasons. The most

important reason is that I truly enjoy mixing my own colors. Developing the palette for each quilt and creating my custom colors by mixing pure hue dyes is truly rewarding. It is also more economical to buy six dyes and mix all your colors from those six than it is to buy dozens of different premixed colors. When you're starting out, it's a good idea to buy about two ounces of each color. The dye in powder form has a long shelf life, and you can replace colors as needed.

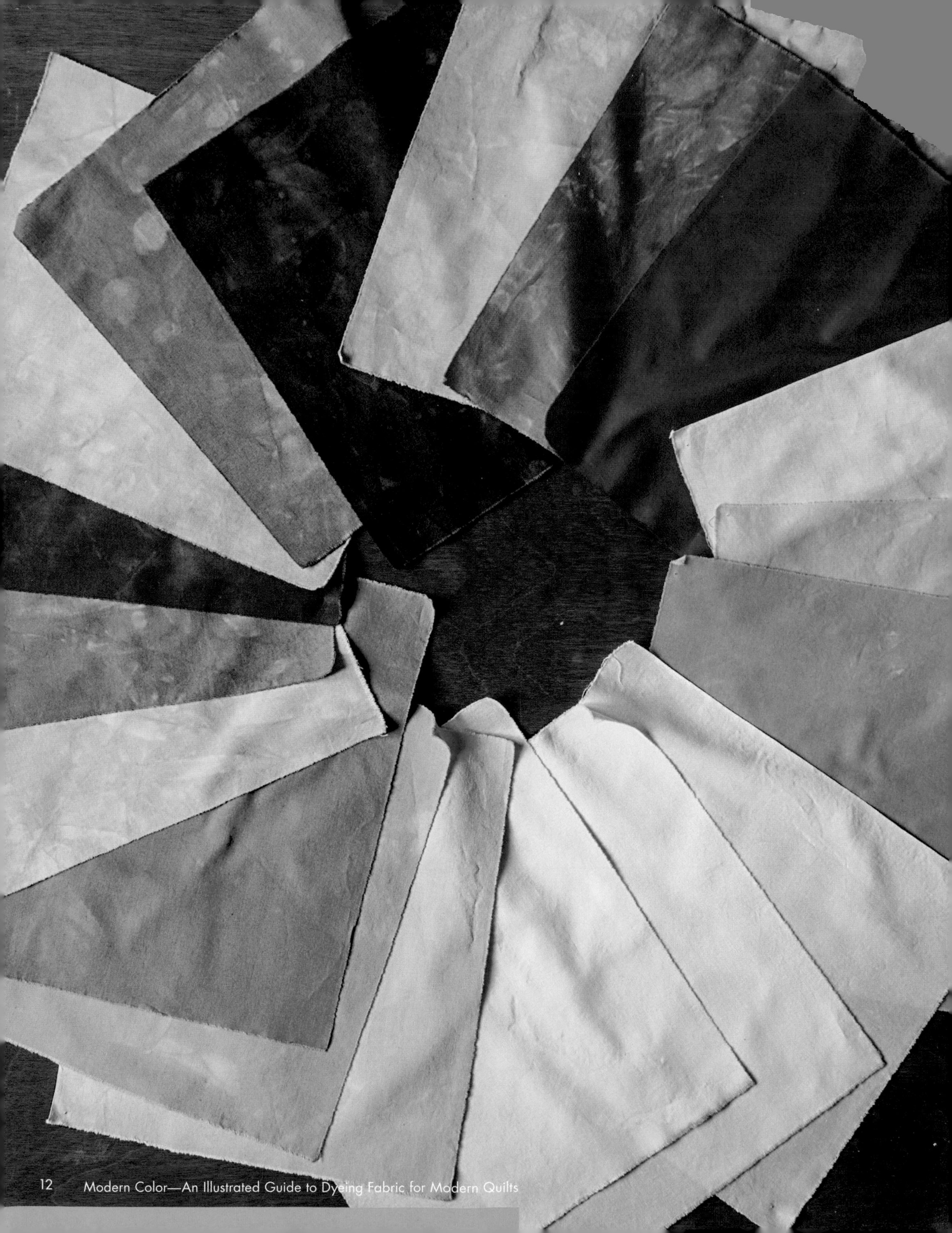

Another benefit of using pure hues is that each hue has a specific Procion code, so although every company names its pure colors differently, the Procion codes are the same. All the fabrics in this book are dyed using different combinations of six different dyes.

NOTE

I usually buy most of my dye and chemicals from Dharma Trading Company, so I will be using those color names.

The first four colors are pure hues: Cerulean Blue, Lemon Yellow, Deep Yellow, and Light Red. I also include two mixed dyes: Khaki and Black. Khaki is Dharma Trading Company's blend, and there isn't an exact equivalent from Pro Chemical & Dye or Jacquard Products. Chino from Pro Chemical & Dye, or Bronze from Jacquard, would be a good substitution. The black dye is a mixture that is consistent between the three companies. The chart below gives the Procion MX code when applicable and the corresponding color names used by each of the three companies.

PROCION MX CODE	DHARMA	PRO CHEMICAL	JACQUARD
Blue MX G	23 Cerulean Blue	406 Intense Blue	070 Cerulean Blue
Yellow MX 8G	1 Lemon Yellow	108 Sun Yellow	004 Lemon Yellow
Yellow MX 3R or Yellow MX 3RA	4 Deep Yellow	104 Golden Yellow	010 Bright Golden Yellow
Red MX 5B	12 Light Red	305 Mixing Red	034 Magenta
	38 Khaki	500n Chino	106 Bronze
Black MX-CWNA	300 New Black	608 Black	128 Warm Black

On page 12: Fabric dyed with (*clockwise from the top*) Light Red, Deep Yellow, Sun Yellow, Cerulean Blue, Khaki, and New Black

FABRIC

Any type of cellulose fabric will work with Procion MX dyes. Fabric that is labeled "mercerized" or "PFD" (prepared for dyeing) will give you the best color results because it has been treated specifically to accept dye. I prefer to use Dharma Trading Company's Mercerized Cotton Print Cloth or Kona Cotton PFD, or Robert Kaufman's PFD Kona Cotton. Regular cotton fabrics such as muslin, quilter's cotton, old cotton sheets, osnaburg, cotton flannel, or regular Kona Cotton are perfectly suitable, but the color will most likely look lighter than it would on mercerized or PFD fabric. All the quilts in this book were made from either Dharma's Mercerized Cotton Print Cloth or Robert Kaufman's PFD Kona Cotton.

DYE AUXILIARIES

Auxiliaries are the extra chemicals you add to a dye bath. Each serves an important purpose.

Dye auxiliaries

Soda Ash (Sodium Carbonate)

Soda ash is used to ensure chemical bonding between the dye and fabric. It is the most important auxiliary because without it the dye will not bond with the fabric, and you will get only a pale color that is neither washfast nor lightfast. Soda ash is a mild alkali and can be irritating to the skin. Gloves and safety glasses should be worn when working with soda ash. It is called Pro Dye Activator by Pro Chemical & Dye or Soda Ash Fixer by Dharma Trading Company.

Salt

Salt helps push the dye into the fabric so you get a more even color. If you forget to add salt, it's not the end of the world unless you want perfectly smooth, even color. If you prefer more mottled, uneven color, you can leave the salt out intentionally. Non-iodized salt is best. I prefer to use pickling salt because it is non-iodized and dissolves quickly in water. Regular table salt will also work.

Water Softener

Water softener is necessary if you have hard water—water that contains minerals such as calcium or magnesium. Hard water can cause spotting on your fabric and can make it difficult to wash out the excess dye. Using a chemical water softener is an inexpensive fix to this problem. Adding a small amount to your dye bath will eliminate any hard-water spotting. Also adding the softener to the final wash-out stage in the washing machine will help get the excess dye out. The name of the softener varies between sellers; what you want is sodium hexametaphosphate. From Dharma Trading Company it is Water Softener, from Pro Chemical & Dye it is Metaphos, and from Jacquard it is Calgon.

NOT SURE IF YOU HAVE HARD WATER?

If you have noticed a white, chalky residue on your dishes after washing them in the dishwasher, or on the inside of your shower or bathtub, you probably have hard water. If you want to make sure, most local hardware stores sell inexpensive home water test kits.

Synthrapol

Synthrapol is a detergent used in prewashing fabric and in washing the fabric after it has been dyed. It can also be used to wash commercially dyed fabrics if you are worried about them bleeding into each other (to avoid the dreaded pink that comes from washing red fabric with white fabric). Dharma Trading Company makes a Synthrapol alternative, called Professional Textile Detergent, which is eco-friendly, nontoxic, and less expensive than Synthrapol.

SETTING UP TO DYE AT HOME

The first step is to gather up all the supplies needed for dyeing fabric. You probably already have some of the items, others you can find at your local craft or hardware store, and some you will need to order online. Below is a complete shopping list of all the items you will need, with descriptions of some of those you may not be familiar with. Each project will give you specific instructions as to the amount of each item needed.

Dye Supplies

Refer to Resources (page 140) for sources of the following supplies.

2 oz. of each dye color listed (page 13)

5 lbs. soda ash

8 lbs. salt

1 qt. Synthrapol or Professional Textile Detergent

1 lb. water softener (if you have hard water; refer to Water Softener, page 15)

Cotton quilting fabric (page 14)

Equipment

Dust mask (for particulates, available in the paint aisle at most hardware stores)

Rubber gloves (regular kitchen dishwashing gloves are perfect)

Plastic safety glasses

Plastic spoons

Measuring cups

Measuring spoons that go to ⅟₃₂ teaspoon*

Old towels for cleanup

Small plastic cups (1-cup-size disposable plastic cups or small yogurt cups for dissolving dye)

Large plastic buckets (such as quart, gallon, 3-gallon, 5-gallon)

Long-handled plastic spoons

Clear plastic box with lid (for measuring dye powder and storage)

Newspaper

Spray bottle filled with water

SAFETY FIRST!

All equipment used for dyeing should be reserved only for dyeing. Never use measuring spoons, cups, or anything else for food after it has touched dye.

* Progressive makes a 19-piece measuring cup and spoon set that is perfect for dyeing. It has every size you could ever want and can be found for around $10 at larger kitchen stores and online retailers such as Amazon.

Dyeing supplies

Dyeing Area

All you need to dye fabric at home is a table and a nearby water source with hot water. If your worktable is nicer than a folding table, or is sometimes used for food, put down a few layers of newspaper or old sheets, a vinyl tablecloth that will only be used for dyeing, or a plastic drop cloth. Also cover the floor if you have a floor that can't easily be wiped up. Basements and garages are perfect for dyeing, but bathrooms are also suitable if you are careful to protect surfaces, keep dye contained, and clean spills immediately.

I keep my dye and auxiliaries (soda ash, salt, Metaphos, and Synthrapol) in a clear plastic box with a lid. When I start dyeing, I take everything out of the box, and the box becomes my dye-measuring station. Turn the box on its side, put a few layers of newspaper in the bottom, and spray the whole thing down with water. The water will attract any stray dye particles so they don't float around the room. Now you can safely measure and dissolve your dye powder inside the box while minimizing the spread of dye particles. When you're done dyeing for the day, throw away the newspaper, rinse and dry the box, and store the dyes and auxiliaries in it for next time.

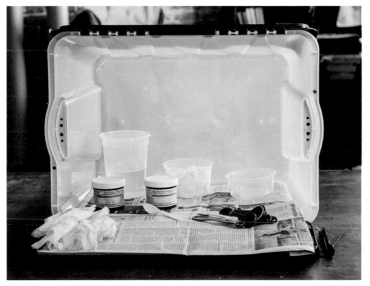

Box set up for measuring dyes

It's best to have a sink nearby, but if you don't it is definitely possible to carry water to your dye area. In my studio, the sink isn't close to my dye station, so I keep a five-gallon bucket nearby and fill it with warm water when I'm getting ready to dye. I use that water to make the dye baths and to soak my fabric. I keep another bucket nearby for containers and spoons that need rinsing, and I throw everything in that bucket until I'm ready to take it to the sink to rinse out.

TIP

Buying soda ash and salt in larger quantities is more economical. Fill a small plastic lidded container with salt and another one with soda ash; be sure to label them. It will be easier to measure from these smaller containers, and you can refill them from your larger supply as needed.

HOW TO DYE FABRIC

The following directions apply to every dye recipe in the book. For each project, you will be given quantities of fabric and amounts of dye needed to make each color. The steps for every color will be the same; the quantities of fabric, water, dye, and auxiliaries will change depending on the amount of each color needed.

Gather all your dyeing supplies and fabric before you start. Always wear rubber gloves when working with dye and auxiliaries, measuring dye powder, stirring dye baths, and washing out fabric. Always wear a dust mask when working with dry dye powder. Once the dye is completely dissolved in water, you can remove the dust mask.

1. Prewash the Fabric

Always prewash any fabric in your washing machine with hot water and laundry detergent or ½ teaspoon Synthrapol and 1 teaspoon soda ash. This will prepare the fabric for dyeing by removing dirt, oils, and sizing. Mercerized or PFD fabrics are ready to dye, but I usually wash them in a bucket of hot water with ½ teaspoon Synthrapol and 1 teaspoon soda ash just in case they have dirt or oils on them from my hands or work surfaces. You can dry your fabric and keep it for later, or keep it wet if you are ready to dye it immediately.

2. Soak the Fabric in Warm Water

Fill up a large bucket with enough warm water so that all the fabric can be submerged and move freely. Let the fabric soak while you are getting everything else ready. This step will help the dye distribute evenly through the fabric for smooth results. When you are ready to dye the fabric, gently squeeze out some of the excess water before adding the fabric to the dye bath.

SAFETY FIRST!

Material Safety Data Sheets (MSDS) are available online from Dharma Trading Company and Pro Chemical & Dye. Powder dye can cause respiratory allergies if inhaled. Always wear your dust mask when working with powdered dyes, and keep the dyes contained by working with them in your dye measuring box and replacing the dye container lid as soon as you are finished with it.

3. Measure and Dissolve the Dye Powder

Measure the required amount of dye powder from the recipe into a small plastic container. Use a clean measuring spoon for each dye color so your dyes don't get contaminated. I keep a little yogurt container filled with water and a towel in my dye-measuring box so I can rinse and dry my measuring spoons in between each color. When all the dyes needed for one color mixture are measured into the container, dissolve the powder in 1 or 2 tablespoons of room-temperature water to create a smooth dye paste. Stir the dye and water well so there are no lumps or specks of dry dye floating on the surface. Set the dissolved dye aside while you prepare the dye bath.

Dissolve dye powder in water.

DYE MIXING TIPS

• Be systematic about measuring dye powder: With your gloves and dust mask on, place the dye container, an empty plastic container, a small container of water, and the measuring spoons in the dye measuring box. Remove the dye lid, measure out the needed dye into the empty container, and immediately replace the lid. Then follow the same procedure for the other dye powders needed to mix a color.

• Clean up any spilled dry or wet dye immediately.

4. Prepare the Dye Bath

Measure the required amount of warm water for the dye bath recipe into a plastic container that will easily hold the water and fabric, leaving plenty of room for stirring. Add the non-iodized salt and stir well to dissolve. If you have hard water, add the required amount of water softener and stir the dye bath well. Then add the dissolved dye from Step 3 and stir well. You can set up multiple dye baths at once, but pay attention to how much water and salt you need for each color, as the amounts might be different.

More dyeing supplies

DON'T FORGET THE SODA ASH!

These two fabrics were dyed the same color, but the lighter one on the left wasn't activated with soda ash.

Without soda ash

With soda ash

TO STIR OR NOT TO STIR?

The mottled green fabric was not stirred much, and the more even-colored fabric was stirred regularly.

Not stirred much

Stirred regularly

5. Add the Fabric to the Dye Bath

Stir the dye bath again and add the damp fabric. For even results, stir regularly for 15 minutes. For mottled or uneven color, you can leave the fabric in the dye bath without stirring or stirring only occasionally.

6. Activate the Dye

At this point the dye has not bonded with the fabric. It is necessary to activate the dye to chemically bond it with the fibers so that you achieve the expected color. This will also make it wash- and lightfast.

To activate the dye, dissolve the required amount of soda ash from your recipe in 2–4 tablespoons of water. Push the fabric to the side of the dye bath with your gloved hand or a long-handled plastic spoon and add the dissolved soda ash to the bath by pouring it down the side, not directly onto the fabric. Stir well. The fabric must remain in the dye bath for at least 30 minutes after the soda ash is added for the dye to fully react with the fibers. For darker colors and black, it is often helpful to leave the fabric in the dye bath for 45 minutes. For the most even color, stir the dye bath regularly during the 30 minutes. For mottled or uneven color, less stirring is required. You can decide which look you prefer.

TIP

If time is an issue, the fabric can be left in the dye bath for longer than 30 to 45 minutes. Stir the fabric occasionally and come back to wash out the fabric (Step 7) when it's convenient.

7. Wash Out the Fabric

Start by rinsing the fabric with cool water until the water runs clear. Gradually increase the water temperature to hot and continue rinsing until the water is clear.

Add a few drops of Synthrapol or Professional Textile Detergent to a container of hot water and swish the fabric for a few minutes. Rinse the fabric again with hot water. Repeat the last two steps until there is no trace of color in the rinse water. Gently squeeze out excess water.

Begin wash process with cold water.

WASHOUT TIPS

• After the initial rinsing with cool water, you can let the fabric soak in warm water with Synthrapol or Professional Textile Detergent for a few hours, until you're ready to finish washing it out. If you are washing very different colors, it is best to separate them out so only similar colors are soaking together.

• Don't let different-colored dyed fabrics lie in a pile during the washout process. Dye can easily transfer from one fabric to another at this stage. Similar colors can be washed out together in the same container of warm soapy water after the initial rinsing with cold water.

• It is very important that you get all the dye out of the fabric, but this takes quite a bit of hand

washing time. I usually wash the fabric out as much as possible and then run it through my washing machine on warm with a tablespoon of Synthrapol or Professional Textile Detergent and an extra rinse cycle. As long as you don't wash a load of whites immediately after this (I wash my rags and towels after a load of hand-dyed fabric), you don't have to worry about any color transferring onto your clothes.

• Fabric is easier to iron smooth if it is damp. If you have the time, iron the fabric after it comes out of the washing machine. Otherwise, dry it in the drier or on a drying rack and spray it with water before ironing.

DYEING GRADATIONS

Several of the projects in this book provide instructions for dyeing gradations—either from a light value to a dark value or from light to dark with an additional color added in. Dyeing gradations is a great way to make sure your fabric stash has a range of values from light to dark. It's also the only way to get subtle increments of value within one color.

The directions for each project that uses gradations include specific instructions to create the dye baths; other than that, the process is exactly the same as described in this chapter.

Dyeing dark to light gradation

DYEING FROM YOUR OWN RECIPES

Each quilt project in this book will specify how much fabric you need in each color and how to make that color. Once you have practiced with my colors and feel comfortable with the process, you will probably want to create your own. I am very picky about color and keep meticulous notes on how to create each color I use so it can be recreated. Other fabric dyers like to wing it and love the surprise of mixing dyes differently each time to see what is possible. Neither method is better than the other, but one will be right for you.

When you are beginning, it's helpful to keep notes on your process, even if you are in the camp of dyers who wing it. I've created a dye recipe card (page 138) that you can photocopy to help you keep track of your own recipes. Make note of how much fabric, how much salt and soda ash, and how much of each dye powder you use. The chart below will you help you get started with quantities.

The dye powder amounts listed are the total amounts needed for pale, medium, or dark colors. You can use the total amount of one color, or combine more than one color to achieve the total amount needed. For example, to mix a pale purple on ½ yard of fabric, I would use ⅛–¼ teaspoon of dye powder total, so ⅛ teaspoon of Cerulean Blue plus ⅛ teaspoon of Light Red might be a good place to start.

	¼ YARD FABRIC	½ YARD FABRIC	1 YARD FABRIC
Dye powder, pale	¹⁄₁₆–⅛ tsp.*	⅛–¼ tsp.	¼–½ tsp.
Dye powder, medium	¼ tsp.	½ tsp.	1–2 tsp.
Dye powder, dark	¾ tsp.	2 tsp.	3–4 tsp.
Water	2 cups	1 qt.	2 qts.
Salt	½ Tbsp.*	1 Tbsp.	2 Tbsp.
Soda ash	½ tsp.	1 tsp.	2 tsp.
Water softener (if needed)	⅛ tsp.	¼ tsp.	½ tsp.

tsp. = teaspoon; Tbsp. = tablespoon

NOTES ON COLOR

• Dye colors do not mix like paint colors. Adding black dye to another color will not make that color more gray like adding black paint does. It is a good way to make a color deeper and richer. I also find it helpful to think of black as a dark gray-blue. Adding it to yellow will give you different greens, and adding it to red will result in purples.

• Some colors are stronger than others, meaning that when you mix them, one color will be more prominent. For example, if you are attempting to mix a true orange, you might mix half yellow with half red. This will result in a very reddish orange. Yellow is a lighter, weaker color and needs to be added in larger quantities to red and blue in order to have a visible effect.

• Remember that there is no such thing as white dye. To achieve very pastel colors, use the smallest measurement of dye needed for the amount of fabric you have.

• Don't judge a color too soon. It is impossible to know exactly how a color will turn out until after the dyed fabric has been washed and dried. A color will often look one way when you first add the fabric to the dye bath and then change after the soda ash is added. It will look much darker in the dye bath than when it is washed and dried.

• Interesting results can be had from overdyeing fabric. If you dye your fabric a color that you're not excited about, it can be put into another dye bath after it has been washed out. The new dye color will overlay the previous color for a new, third color. Think of your color wheel here: yellow fabric overdyed with blue will result in green fabric.

• Quilt backs are great places to test out your own color recipes. I love surprising colors on the backs of quilts—especially quilts that are meant to live on a wall.

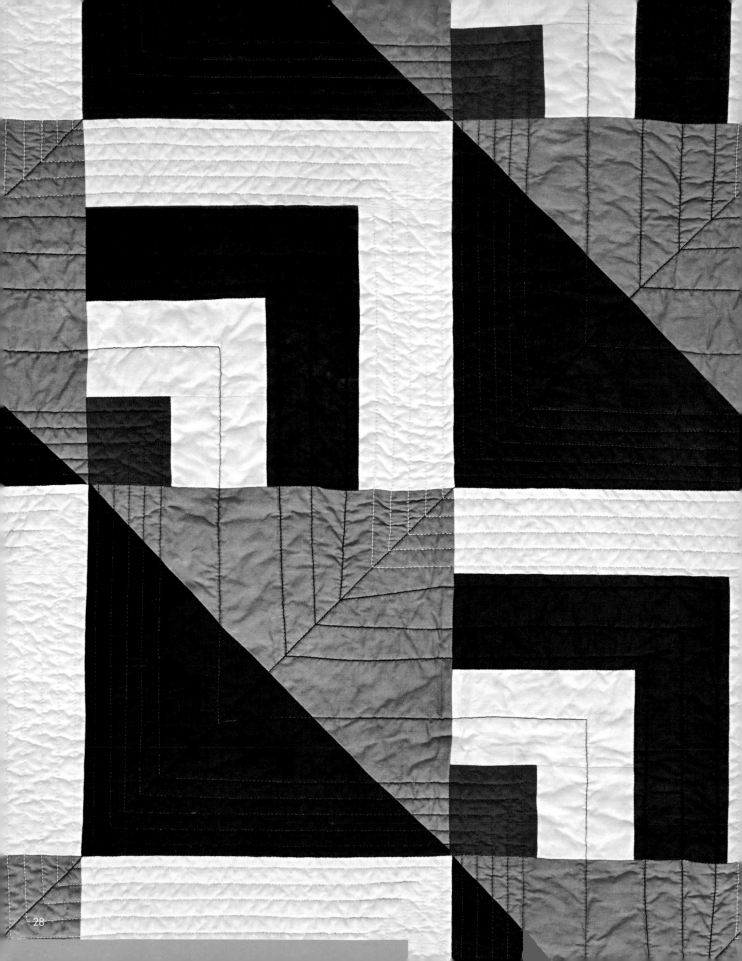

PROJECTS

I love quilts. I love looking at them, thinking about them, reading about them, talking about them, sleeping under them, and most of all making them. The steps involved in quilting are very straightforward, but they leave plenty of room for improvisation or new techniques.

If you are new to quiltmaking, please refer to Resources (page 140) for comprehensive books on quiltmaking. If you have made some quilts before and have your own methods of doing things, all the techniques you already use work just the same when you are using your own hand-dyed fabric.

I LOVE QUILTS. I LOVE LOOKING
AT THEM, THINKING ABOUT THEM,
READING ABOUT THEM, TALKING ABOUT
THEM, SLEEPING UNDER THEM, AND
MOST OF ALL MAKING THEM.

You will follow the same basic guidelines for each quilt in the book. While you're working, remember that craftsmanship is important. All the steps involved in making a quilt take practice to perfect. Being off even a little on your cutting or seams can add up to a big difference in the finished quilt. Taking the time to rip out seams and resew them if they're wrong will pay off in the end. At the same time, don't worry too much if things don't line up perfectly or are slightly wonky. Quiltmaking should be a pleasure, not drudgery. Small mistakes or wonky areas will add to the character of your quilt.

If you want to start with something small, try the *Dip-Dyed Place Mats* (page 30) or the *Quilted Zipper Clutch/Tablet Case* (page 34), or you can jump right into making any of the quilts.

When you're ready to dive into selecting and mixing your own colors using your own inspiration, you've graduated to making a striped landscape quilt (page 112).

DIP-DYED PLACE MATS

FINISHED PLACE MATS: set of 4, each 19″ × 14″

I love to make place mats when I'm trying out new dyeing techniques, and these are perfect if you've never dyed fabric before. They don't require a lot of fabric—a set of four needs only a yard of fabric for the front and a yard for the back. The construction is simple and doesn't require any binding, so they're fast and fun to make. I also think place mats make great gifts.

Who doesn't love getting something unique and handmade to brighten up their home?

You can make yours one-sided like I did, with dip-dyed fabric on the front and coordinating solids on the back, or make them reversible, with two different and exciting fabrics on the front and back.

MATERIALS

Yardage is based on 44″-wide fabric. Makes 4 place mats.

- 1 yard undyed white fabric for the fronts

- Backing: 1 yard undyed white fabric *or* any other fabric you have

- Batting: 4 pieces 22″ × 17″

DYEING EQUIPMENT AND INSTRUCTIONS

The basic idea of dip dyeing is that the fabric is folded into a bundle and one edge of the bundle is dipped into dye so that the dye will wick up into the fabric. If the fabric is dry when it's dipped, the wicking effect will be soft and even, most likely with a halo effect, as you can see in the project photo, at right.

This place mat was dip dyed using a dry fabric bundle two separate times to create the grid effect. Follow the instructions or experiment with different folding techniques and your own color recipes. Use whichever dipping method (wet or dry) you prefer.

Dye Bath #1

Refer to How to Dye Fabric (page 20) as needed.

1. Accordion fold 1 yard of fabric. Each fold should be about 2″–3″ wide. Loosely roll the folded fabric into a cinnamon-roll shape. Do not wet this fabric, as you will be dry dipping the bundle into the dye bath (Figure A).

2. Dissolve 1½ teaspoons Cerulean Blue and 1½ teaspoons New Black in 1 cup warm water.

3. Pour the dissolved dye into a somewhat shallow 1-quart container—you will want the dye to come about halfway up the roll of fabric.

4. Stir in 1 teaspoon soda ash.

5. Gently place the dry cinnamon roll–shaped bundle of fabric into the dye so that an edge

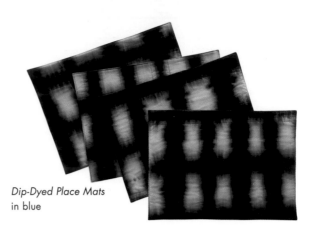

Dip-Dyed Place Mats in blue

of folds is submerged but the top is not in the dye. Slightly loosen the cinnamon-roll shape so that dye can get in between all the layers (Figures B and C).

6. Leave the fabric in the dye for 30 minutes.

7. Wash out the fabric (page 23) and then iron the fabric until dry.

8. Discard any remaining dye solution.

A. Accordion fold fabric; then roll.

B. Place fabric roll in dye.

C. Dye wicking into layers

Dye Bath #2

1. Accordion fold the dry fabric perpendicular to the blue stripes. Loosely roll the folded fabric into a cinnamon-roll shape again.

2. Dissolve ½ teaspoon Cerulean Blue and ½ teaspoon New Black in 1 cup warm water.

3. Pour the dissolved dye into the shallow 1-quart container.

4. Follow Steps 4–8 of dye bath #1 (page 32).

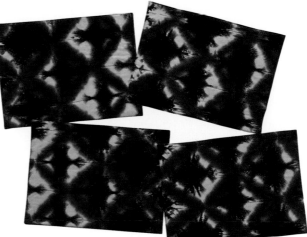

Gold and black *Dip-Dyed Place Mats*

TIP

In this gold and black version, the fabric bundles were folded using an *itajime shibori* folding technique similar to that used in the *Quilted Shibori Wallhanging* (page 100). They were accordion folded, then folded into a triangle bundle. The base of the dry fabric triangle was dipped in the gold color. Then it was washed out and refolded the same way, and the tip of the now wet triangle bundle was dipped in black dye. If the fabric is wet when dipped, it will wick more dramatically and create interesting splotches and veinlike markings.

PLACE MAT BACKING

For the backing, I used an assortment of scrap fabrics. If you want a coordinating color for the backs, you can dissolve the same amount of dye from either dye bath #1 or #2 in a few tablespoons of warm water and dye 1 yard of fabric a solid color by referring to How to Dye Fabric (page 20).

PLACE MAT ASSEMBLY

1. Cut the top fabric into 4 pieces, each 22″ × 17″.

2. Cut 4 pieces of backing fabric, each 20″ × 15″. Set the backing pieces aside.

3. Layer a piece of top fabric, right side up, on top of a 22″ × 17″ piece of batting. Baste with safety pins. Repeat for the remaining 3 pieces of top fabric and 3 pieces of batting.

4. Quilt the basted place mat pieces.

5. Trim the quilted place mat tops to 20″ × 15″.

6. With right sides together, layer each piece of backing fabric with a quilted place mat top. Pin the edges all around.

7. Sew the edges with a ½″ seam allowance, leaving a few inches open on a short end.

8. Clip the corners and turn the place mats right side out. Push out the corners to make them square and iron the place mats well.

9. Make sure the edge that was left open is turned inside neatly; then topstitch close to the edge all the way around, backstitching at the beginning and the end.

QUILTED ZIPPER CLUTCH/TABLET CASE

FINISHED CLUTCH: 11″ × 8½″

This quilted zipper clutch is a very convenient size. It is the perfect size to use as an iPad (or other tablet) case. Or throw in your wallet, phone, keys, and lip balm; fold over the top; and use it as a clutch. Everyone who sees it will be totally jealous that you have such great taste, and they will be in awe of your mad dyeing and quilting skills.

If you've never put in a zipper before, relax—this one is a cinch!

MATERIALS AND EQUIPMENT

Yardage is based on 44″-wide fabric.

- 1 fat quarter white fabric for the outside

- 1 fat quarter (dyed or undyed) fabric for the lining (This is a good place to use your "mistakes.")

- Batting: 2 pieces 11″ × 13″

- 10″ zipper to coordinate with the dyed outside fabric

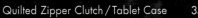

DYEING EQUIPMENT AND INSTRUCTIONS

Some of my favorite fabrics are those I've dyed using the technique for mottled color. I don't normally use those fabrics in my quilts because most of the time they are too bright and busy for my clean, graphic aesthetic. But they're so pretty! So I use them in these bags. That way I get to look at them frequently and admire the color blending, but they don't distract from my quilt designs. Win-win!

Refer to How to Dye Fabric (page 20) as needed.

1. Soak the fabric in warm water for a few minutes while you dissolve the dye powder.

2. Choose 2 or 3 colors to make into dye solutions (more than 3 will get too muddy). You can mix dye colors or use them straight out of the container. One color is a nice choice if you prefer a monochromatic look. Dissolve ⅛–½ teaspoon dye powder in ¼ cup warm water. Do this for each of the colors that you chose.

3. Squeeze out some of the extra water from the fabric and put the fabric into a dry container. The size of the container will determine how much mottling is on the fabric. The smaller the container, the more mottling and distinct areas of color you will have. With a bigger container, you will get more color mixing and potentially less mottling.

4. Pour some of each dye solution over the fabric. You can try to keep the dye areas separate or overlap them to create mixtures. You may or may not use all the dye solutions.

Pour dye on fabric.

5. Decide how mottled you want the fabric to be. If you want it very mottled, leave it alone. If you want more subtle mixtures and less white areas, poke the fabric with your gloved hand a few times, or pick up the fabric and gently squeeze or turn it over in the container. The more you handle the fabric, the more the colors will blend.

TIP

It is fun to do more than one piece of fabric at a time with the same colors. Use a separate container for each piece of fabric. Then pour the dye over each piece, using the same colors of dye solution. Handle each piece of fabric differently to see what variety you can achieve. Leave one alone, gently poke one a couple of times, and squeeze another repeatedly. You will be surprised by how different the fabrics will look.

For more blending, poke fabric and turn it over.

6. Dissolve ¼ teaspoon soda ash in a few tablespoons of water. Pour the soda ash over the dyed fabric. Again, you can leave the fabric alone at this point for maximum mottling, or you can poke it or squeeze it a couple of times. Let the soda ash and dye work on the fabric for 30 minutes.

7. Wash out the fabric (page 23).

CUTTING INSTRUCTIONS

- From the dyed outer fabric:

  Cut 2 pieces 11″ × 13″.

- From the lining fabric

  Cut 2 pieces 9½″ × 11½″.

CONSTRUCTION

1. Layer each piece of dyed outer fabric right side up on top of an 11″ × 13″ piece of batting.

2. Using safety pins, baste each piece of dyed outer fabric to the piece of quilt batting. Then quilt as desired.

3. Trim the quilted layers to 9½″ × 11½″.

4. Place a quilted layer fabric side up. Place the zipper face down along a short edge of the quilted layer as shown. Place the zipper on the short edge of the quilted section with the top edge of the zipper tape and the top edge of the quilted section even with each other.

Place zipper on short edge.

5. Place the lining fabric directly on top of the quilted layer and zipper, aligning all 4 edges. Pin along the edge with the zipper as shown.

Pin zipper between quilted layer and lining.

6. Open the zipper about halfway. Using a zipper foot, backstitch at one end of the zipper edge and continue sewing. Sew with the inner edge of the zipper foot close to the zipper teeth. When the stitching gets close to the zipper tab, stop sewing with the needle down. Lift the presser foot and gently pull the zipper tab back and out of the way. Then lower the presser foot and continue sewing. Backstitch at the end.

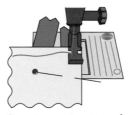

Sew zipper using zipper foot.

7. Turn the lining fabric to the back so that the wrong side of the lining fabric is lined up with the quilt batting on the quilted layer.

8. Repeat Steps 6 and 7 with the other quilted layer and lining piece on the other side of the zipper. Note that the first pieces you sewed together will be between the new quilted layer and lining sandwich. When the stitching is complete, turn the layers right side up as shown.

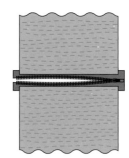

Pin and sew zipper to other side.

Zipper sewn on both sides

9. Open the zipper about halfway again. Align the right sides of the quilted layers together and the right sides of the lining layers together. Pin around the edges. Make sure the zipper ends are facing toward the lining.

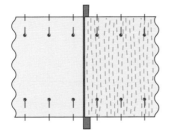

Pin together edges.

10. Sew around the outer edge, using a ¼″ seam allowance and leaving about a 4″ opening in the middle of the bottom edge of the lining layer. Sew back and forth over the zipper ends a couple of times for extra strength. Backstitch at the beginning and the end.

11. Clip off the corners and the extra zipper tape.

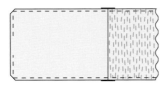

Clip corners.

12. To turn the clutch right side out, reach up through the lining and grab the quilted layers. Pull them through the open zipper and

out the hole in the lining. Push the corners out to make them as square as possible.

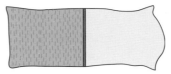

Turn right side out.

13. Press each side well and sew along the bottom edge of the lining to close up the hole.

14. Push the lining inside the clutch and you are done!

Finished!

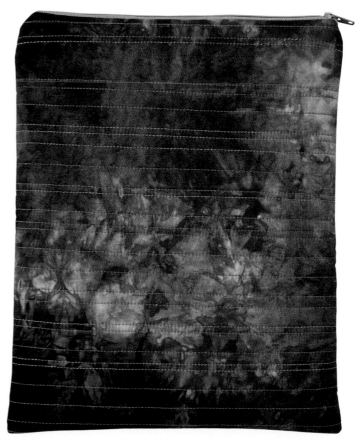

STEP QUILT

FINISHED BLOCK: 10˝ × 10˝

FINISHED QUILT: 40˝ × 50˝ for crib size, 66˝ × 86˝ for twin size

I visited the International Quilt Study Center and Museum in Lincoln, Nebraska, in the fall of 2010. The experience as a whole was amazing, but an exhibition called *South Asian Seams: Quilts from India, Pakistan, and Bangladesh* particularly affected me. The quilts were bold, with dynamic compositions and striking color combinations. Some of them were intricately cut and appliquéd like *scherenschnitte* (cut paper) quilts, while others had thousands of colorful stitches covering the surface. The quilts that I kept going back to look at combined highly contrasting colors with patterns I recognized from traditional American quilts, such as Log Cabin, but in different arrangements. The *Step Quilt* is inspired by one of these quilts— a traditional *ralli* quilt from the middle Sindh region of Pakistan. The red and black version of the quilt is more in tune with the colors traditionally used in ralli quilts, while the blue and gray version is meant to be softer and more visually calming.

As an introduction to dyeing, this quilt is a great place to start. Each version has only three colors to dye, so it's easy to keep track of what you're doing.

MATERIALS AND EQUIPMENT

Yardage is based on 44˝-wide fabric.

	CRIB SIZE	TWIN SIZE
WHITE (UNDYED) FABRIC	5¼ yards*	13¼ yards*
BATTING	44˝ × 54˝	72˝ × 92˝
BUCKETS	One 1-quart size, three 1-gallon size, and one 2- or 3-gallon size	Two 1-gallon size and four 2- or 3-gallon size

* Note: If you want to dye fabric for only part of the quilt, refer to the project charts (pages 43 and 46) for the amount of fabric needed for each part.

Crib-size *Step Quilt* in red and black

COLOR RECIPES

Follow the procedure outlined in How to Dye Fabric (page 20) for each dye bath. The fabric for the quilt top is dyed separately from the binding and backing, even though some of the colors are the same. It is a little more work to do this, but it's easier to achieve even dye results because you have less fabric in the dye bath.

TIP

As with all hand-dyed fabric, it is extremely important that you wash out all the extra dye at the end of the dyeing process. With the red and black version of this quilt, it is extra important. If the red fabric isn't completely washed out, you will end up with pink logs instead of white the first time you wash your quilt. I always soak my red fabric again in hot water and a little Synthrapol or Professional Textile Detergent after the final wash in the washing machine.

RED AND BLACK—CRIB SIZE

FABRIC		WATER	BUCKET	SALT	DYE	SODA ASH
RED	¼ yard	2 cups	1-quart	½ Tbsp.*	¼ + ⅛ tsp.* Light Red; ¼ + ⅛ tsp. Deep Yellow	½ tsp.
BLACK	1¼ yards	2¾ quarts	1-gallon	2½ Tbsp.	2 tsp. New Black; 2 tsp. Khaki	1 Tbsp.
CHARTREUSE	¾ yard	1½ quarts	1-gallon	1½ Tbsp.	1½ tsp. Deep Yellow; 1/16 + 1/32 tsp. Cerulean Blue; 1/16 + 1/32 tsp. New Black	1½ tsp.
WHITE (UNDYED)	¾ yard					
RED BINDING	½ yard	1 quart	1-gallon	1 Tbsp.	½ + ¼ tsp. Light Red; ½ + ¼ tsp. Deep Yellow	1 tsp.
BLACK BACKING	1⅝ yards	3 quarts	2- or 3-gallon	3 Tbsp.	2½ tsp. New Black; 2½ tsp. Khaki	3 tsp.

tsp. = teaspoon; Tbsp. = tablespoon

RED AND BLACK—TWIN SIZE

FABRIC		WATER	BUCKET	SALT	DYE	SODA ASH
RED	½ yard	1 quart	1-gallon	1 Tbsp.*	¾ tsp.* Light Red; ¾ tsp. Deep Yellow	1 tsp.
BLACK	2¾ yards	6 quarts	2- or 3-gallon	5½ Tbsp.	2 Tbsp. New Black; 2 Tbsp. Khaki	5½ tsp.
CHARTREUSE	1½ yards	3 quarts	2- or 3-gallon	3 Tbsp.	1 Tbsp. Deep Yellow; ⅛ + 1/16 tsp. Cerulean Blue; ⅛ + 1/16 tsp. New Black	3 tsp.
WHITE (UNDYED)	2¼ yards					
RED BINDING	¾ yard	1½ quarts	1-gallon	1½ Tbsp.	1 tsp. Light Red; 1 tsp. Deep Yellow	1½ tsp.
BLACK BACKING	2¼ yards	5 quarts	2- or 3-gallon	¼ cup	2 Tbsp. New Black; 2 Tbsp. Khaki	4½ tsp.
CHARTREUSE BACKING	2¼ yards	5 quarts	2- or 3-gallon	¼ cup	4 tsp. Deep Yellow; ¼ tsp. Cerulean Blue; ¼ tsp. New Black	4½ tsp.
WHITE (UNDYED) BACKING	¾ yard					

tsp. = teaspoon; Tbsp. = tablespoon

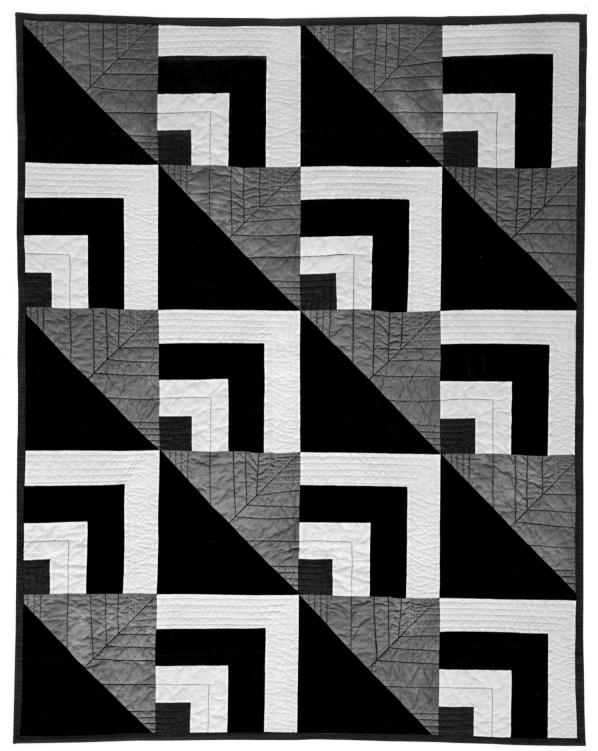

Crib-size *Step Quilt* in red and black

Crib-size *Step Quilt* in blue and gray

BLUE AND GRAY—CRIB SIZE

FABRIC		WATER	BUCKET	SALT	DYE	SODA ASH
GREEN	¼ yard	2 cups	1-quart	½ Tbsp.*	½ tsp.* Cerulean Blue; ½ tsp. Lemon Yellow	½ tsp.
BLUE	1¼ yards	2¾ quarts	1-gallon	2½ Tbsp.	¼ + ¹⁄₃₂ tsp. Cerulean Blue; ¹⁄₃₂ tsp. New Black; ¹⁄₃₂ tsp. Light Red	1 Tbsp.
GRAY	¾ yard	1½ quarts	1-gallon	1½ Tbsp.	¼ + ⅛ tsp. New Black; ⅛ tsp. Khaki	1½ tsp.
WHITE (UNDYED)	¾ yard					
GREEN BINDING	½ yard	1 quart	1-gallon	1 Tbsp.	1 tsp. Cerulean Blue; 1 tsp. Lemon Yellow	1 tsp.
GRAY BACKING	1⅝ yards	3¼ quarts	2- or 3-gallon	3 Tbsp.	½ + ¼ tsp. New Black; ¼ tsp. Khaki	3 tsp.

tsp. = teaspoon; Tbsp. = tablespoon

BLUE AND GRAY—TWIN SIZE

FABRIC		WATER	BUCKET	SALT	DYE	SODA ASH
GREEN	½ yard	1 quart	1-gallon	1 Tbsp.*	1¼ tsp.* Cerulean Blue; 1¼ tsp. Lemon Yellow	1 tsp.
BLUE	2¾ yards	6 quarts	2- or 3-gallon	5½ Tbsp.	¾ tsp. Cerulean Blue; ¹⁄₁₆ tsp. Light Red; ¹⁄₁₆ tsp. New Black	5½ tsp.
GRAY	1½ yards	3 quarts	2- or 3-gallon	3 Tbsp.	¾ tsp. New Black; ¼ tsp. Khaki	3 tsp.
WHITE (UNDYED)	2¼ yards					
GREEN BINDING	¾ yard	1½ quarts	1-gallon	1½ Tbsp.	1¼ tsp. Cerulean Blue; 1¼ tsp. Lemon Yellow	1½ tsp.
BLUE BACKING	2¼ yards	5 quarts	2- or 3-gallon	4 Tbsp.	½ tsp. Cerulean Blue; ¹⁄₁₆ tsp. New Black; ¹⁄₁₆ tsp. Light Red	4½ tsp.
GRAY BACKING	2¼ yards	5 quarts	2- or 3-gallon	4 Tbsp.	1 tsp. New Black; ½ tsp. Khaki	4½ tsp.
WHITE (UNDYED) BACKING	¾ yard					

tsp. = teaspoon; Tbsp. = tablespoon

Crib-size *Step Quilt* in blue and gray

CUTTING INSTRUCTIONS

- From red (or green for blue and gray version):

  FOR CRIB SIZE: Cut 10 squares 3″ × 3″.

  FOR TWIN SIZE: Cut 24 squares 3″ × 3″.

- From white:

  FOR BOTH SIZES: Cut the entire piece of white into strips 3″ × width of fabric.

- From black (or blue for blue and gray version):

  FOR CRIB SIZE: Cut 5 squares 11″ × 11″.

  FOR TWIN SIZE: Cut 12 squares 11″ × 11″.

  FOR BOTH SIZES: Cut the remaining fabric into strips 3″ × width of fabric.

- From chartreuse (or gray for blue and gray version):

  FOR CRIB SIZE: Cut 5 squares 11″ × 11″.

  FOR TWIN SIZE: Cut 12 squares 11″ × 11″.

- From binding fabric:

  FOR CRIB SIZE: Cut 6 strips 2½″ × width of fabric.

  FOR TWIN SIZE: Cut 9 strips 2½″ × width of fabric.

CONSTRUCTION

Seam allowances are ¼″.

Block Assembly

Note: Instructions are written for the red and black version, with colors for the blue and gray version given in parentheses.

HALF-SQUARE TRIANGLE BLOCKS

Make 10 half-square triangle blocks for the crib quilt and make 24 half-square triangle blocks for the twin quilt.

1. Draw a diagonal line from corner to corner on the wrong side of all the chartreuse (gray) 11″ × 11″ squares.

2. With right sides together, place a chartreuse (gray) 11″ × 11″ square on top of a black (blue) 11″ × 11″ square, matching all the sides evenly. Pin along the drawn line, with the pins perpendicular to the line. Sew a scant ¼″ seam on each side of the diagonal line (Figure A).

3. Cut on the diagonal line. Each pair of 11″ squares will make 2 blocks. Open each block and press the seams open. Repeat with the remaining half-square triangle blocks (Figure B).

4. Trim the half-square triangle blocks to 10½″ × 10½″ and trim off any dog-ears.

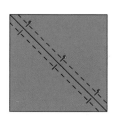

A. Stack, pin, and stitch squares.

B. Cut and press seams open.

HALF–LOG CABIN BLOCKS

Make 10 Half–Log Cabin blocks for the crib quilt and make 24 Half–Log Cabin blocks for the twin.

1. Sew the 3″ red (green) squares to a 3″-wide strip of white, leaving a little space between the red squares (Figure A).

2. Cut apart the blocks, trim them even, and press the seams open.

3. Sew each red and white unit (green and white unit) to another 3″-wide strip of white, leaving a little space between the units. Cut apart the blocks, trim them even, and press the seams open (Figure B). (*Note: These step illustrations do not show the seam allowances from the back of the sewn sections.*)

4. With right sides together, sew each red and white unit (green and white unit) to a 3″-wide strip of black (blue) fabric, leaving a little space between the units. The side with the shorter white strip will be sewn to the black (blue) fabric. Cut the blocks apart, trim them even, and press the seams open (Figure C).

5. Repeat with another strip of black (blue) fabric on the other side of the Half–Log Cabin (Figure D).

6. Sew 2 more rounds of logs using 3″-wide strips of white fabric (Figure E). Refer to the blocks in the quilt assembly diagrams (page 50) if you get lost.

7. Square up and trim the blocks to 10½″ × 10½″ if necessary.

A. Sew squares to white strip.

B. Sew units from Step 2 to white strip.

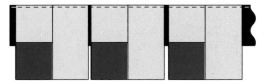

C. Sew units from Step 3 to strip.

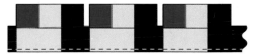

D. Sew unit from Step 4 to strip.

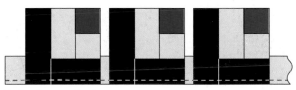

E. Continue sewing logs.

Quilt Assembly

Refer to the quilt photos (pages 44 and 45) and to the quilt assembly diagrams, at right.

For the crib size:

1. Sew together the blocks into 5 rows of 4 blocks each, following the crib quilt assembly diagram. Press the seams open.

2. Sew together the rows. Press the seams open.

For the twin size:

1. Sew together the blocks into 8 rows of 6 blocks each, following the twin quilt assembly diagram. Press the seams open.

2. Sew together the rows. Press the seams open.

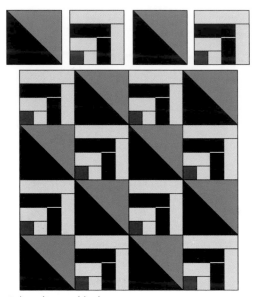

Crib quilt assembly diagram

Borders

For the twin size:

1. Sew the 3˝-wide strips of black (blue) together as if you were making binding strips (page 132) to make a strip that is 65½˝ long and another 80½˝ long.

2. Do the same with the white fabric.

3. Sew the 3˝ × 80½˝ strip of white to the left side of the quilt and the 3˝ × 80½˝ strip of black (blue) to the right side. Press the seams toward the borders.

4. Sew the black (blue) 65½˝ strip to the top and the white 65½˝ strip to the bottom. Press the seams toward the borders.

Twin quilt assembly diagram

Backing

For the crib size:

Trim the backing to approximately 44″ × 54″.

For the twin size:

1. Iron the 3 pieces of fabric listed in the materials section for the backing.

2. Square up all the cut ends of the dyed fabrics and trim off the selvages so you have clean lines for piecing.

3. Cut each dyed piece 72″ × width of fabric.

4. Cut the white fabric into 2 pieces 12″ × 40″. Sew them together along the 12″ sides. Press the seam open and trim the piece to 72″ long.

5. Referring to the twin quilt backing diagram, sew the 3 pieces together, with the white piece in the middle. Press the seams open.

Twin quilt backing diagram

FINISHING

Refer to Quiltmaking Basics: Finishing (page 130) to layer, quilt, and bind the quilt.

CIRCLE QUILT

FINISHED BLOCK: 20″ × 20″
FINISHED QUILT: 20″ × 20″ for pillow, 60″ × 60″ for throw, 86″ × 96″ for queen size

This *Circle Quilt* is my take on the traditional Drunkard's Path pattern. If you haven't noticed already, I like quilts that are bold, graphic, and organized. Don't get me wrong—the traditional Drunkard's Path, and its many variations, is a stunning quilt. But I find myself being drawn to the parts of the pattern that form a full circle. So why not make a quilt that is just circles? Why not, indeed.

The two versions of this quilt use different types of gradation. The peach and green version uses a monochromatic (one color) gradation, while the blue and orange version uses a shade gradation. Adding white to a color is called a tint, and adding black to a color is called a shade. There is no such thing as white dye, but adding black to a color is a great way to deepen it. You will be starting with pure Cerulean Blue and adding black in increasing amounts to create your shade sequence.

Both of these quilts also use complementary color schemes—colors that are opposite each other on the color wheel. Combining complementary colors in a quilt can be very dynamic, as the two colors visually vibrate against each other.

MATERIALS AND EQUIPMENT

Yardage is based on 44″-wide fabric.

	PILLOW	THROW	QUEEN SIZE
WHITE (UNDYED) FABRIC	4½ yards*	12¼ yards*	22½ yards*
BATTING	24″ × 24″	66″ × 66″	92″ × 102″
PILLOW FORM	20″ × 20″		
BUCKETS—FOR BLUE AND ORANGE VERSION	Seven 1-quart size	Six 1-gallon size and one 2- or 3-gallon size	Seven 2- or 3-gallon size and two 1-gallon size
BUCKETS—FOR PEACH AND GREEN VERSION	Seven 1-quart size and two 1-gallon size	Six 1-gallon size and three 2- or 3-gallon size	Eight 2- or 3-gallon size, two 1-gallon size, and one 5-gallon size

* Note: If you want to dye fabric for only part of the quilt, refer to the project charts (pages 55, 56, 58, and 60) for the amount of fabric needed for each part.

The fabric requirements for the throw and the queen-size quilt allow enough extra fabric to also make the top of the pillow. If you are making the throw or the queen-size quilt and also wish to make the pillow, you need to dye only the fabric for the pillow binding and envelope closure.

Queen-size *Circle Quilt*
in blue and orange

COLOR RECIPES

The orange (for the orange and blue version) and the green and gray (for the peach and green version) are dyed as described in How to Dye Fabric (page 20).

Both versions of this quilt also use a gradation. The setup for each dye bath is the same as for a nongradation, but the difference is in how the dye is measured and added to the dye bath. For the blue and orange version of this quilt, there is an added step, as it is a shade sequence instead of a monochromatic sequence. This means you will be starting with a consistent value of Cerulean Blue dye in each of your dye baths and adding increasing amounts of black to them.

NOTES

- You will be making dye solutions for the gradations, so make sure you read through all the gradation instructions (page 62) before you set up the dye baths.

- For both throws and both queen-size quilts, you will be using the leftover backing fabric as binding.

BLUE AND ORANGE—PILLOW

FABRIC		WATER	BUCKETS	SALT	DYE	SODA ASH
BLUE 5-STEP GRADATION	5 pieces ⅓ yard each	2 cups each	Five 1-quart	½ Tbsp.* each	Dye solution 1 = 1 tsp.* Cerulean Blue dissolved in 5 Tbsp. water; Dye solution 2 = ¾ tsp. New Black dissolved in ¼ cup water	½ tsp. each
ORANGE	¼ yard	2 cups	One 1-quart	1½ tsp.	¹⁄₁₆ tsp. Deep Yellow; ¹⁄₃₂ tsp. Lemon Yellow; ¹⁄₃₂ tsp. Light Red	½ tsp.
WHITE (UNDYED) BACKGROUND	¾ yard					
WHITE (UNDYED) PILLOW BACK	1½ yards					

tsp. = teaspoon; Tbsp. = tablespoon

Circle Quilt pillow in blue and orange

BLUE AND ORANGE—THROW

FABRIC		WATER	BUCKETS	SALT	DYE	SODA ASH
BLUE 5-STEP GRADATION	5 pieces 1 yard each	2 quarts each	Five 1-gallon	2 Tbsp.* each	Dye solution 1 = 3¾ tsp.* Cerulean Blue dissolved in 5 Tbsp. water; Dye solution 2 = 4 tsp. New Black dissolved in ¼ cup water	2 tsp. each
ORANGE	¾ yard	1½ quarts	One 1-gallon	1½ Tbsp.	¼ + ⅛ tsp. Deep Yellow; ⅛ + 1/16 tsp. Lemon Yellow; ⅛ + 1/16 tsp. Light Red	1½ tsp.
WHITE (UNDYED) BACKGROUND	2½ yards					
ORANGE BACKING AND BINDING	2 yards	4 quarts	One 2- or 3-gallon	4 Tbsp.	¾ tsp. Deep Yellow; ¼ + ⅛ tsp. Lemon Yellow; ¼ + ⅛ tsp. Light Red	4 tsp.
WHITE (UNDYED) BACKING	2 yards					

tsp. = teaspoon; Tbsp. = tablespoon

BLUE AND ORANGE—QUEEN SIZE

FABRIC		WATER	BUCKETS	SALT	DYE	SODA ASH
BLUE 5-STEP GRADATION	5 pieces 1¾ yards each	3½ quarts each	Five 2- or 3-gallon	4 Tbsp.* each	Dye solution 1 = 2 Tbsp. + ¼ tsp.* Cerulean Blue dissolved in 5 Tbsp. water; Dye solution 2 = 5⅛ tsp. New Black dissolved in ¼ cup water	4 tsp. each
ORANGE	1¼ yards	2¾ quarts	One 1-gallon	2½ Tbsp.	¼ + ⅛ tsp. Deep Yellow; ⅛ + 1/16 tsp. Lemon Yellow; ⅛ + 1/16 tsp. Light Red	1 Tbsp.
WHITE (UNDYED) BACKGROUND	4 yards					
ORANGE BORDER	1 yard	2 quarts	One 1-gallon	2 Tbsp.	¼ + ⅛ tsp. Deep Yellow; ⅛ + 1/16 tsp. Lemon Yellow; ⅛ + 1/16 tsp. Light Red	2 tsp.
ORANGE BACKING AND BINDING	2½ yards	5 quarts	One 2- or 3-gallon	5 Tbsp.	1 tsp. Deep Yellow; ½ tsp. Lemon Yellow; ½ tsp. Light Red	5 tsp.
BLUE BACKING	2½ yards	5 quarts	One 2- or 3-gallon	5 Tbsp.	1¾ tsp. Cerulean Blue; ¼ tsp. New Black	5 tsp.
WHITE (UNDYED) BACKING	2½ yards					

tsp. = teaspoon; Tbsp. = tablespoon

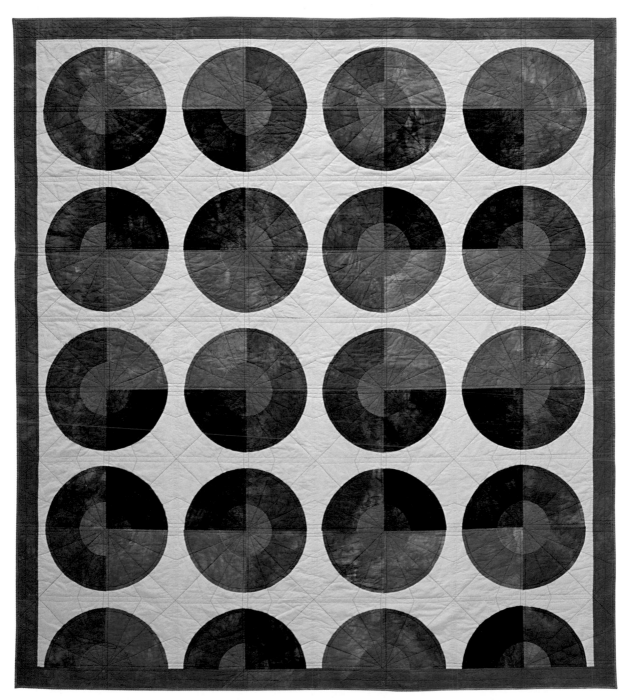

Queen-size *Circle Quilt* in blue and orange

PEACH AND GREEN—PILLOW

FABRIC		WATER	BUCKETS	SALT	DYE	SODA ASH
PEACH 5-STEP GRADATION	5 pieces ⅓ yard each	2 cups each	Five 1-quart	½ Tbsp.* each	Dye solution = ¼ tsp.* Light Red, ¼ + ⅛ tsp. Deep Yellow, and ¹⁄₁₆ tsp. Khaki dissolved in ¼ cup water	½ tsp. each
GREEN	¼ yard	2 cups	One 1-quart	½ Tbsp.	⅛ tsp. Cerulean Blue; ¹⁄₁₆ tsp. Lemon Yellow	½ tsp.
GRAY	¾ yard	1½ quarts	One 1-gallon	1½ Tbsp.	⅜ tsp. New Black; ⅜ tsp. Khaki	1½ tsp.
GRAY PILLOW BACKING	1½ yards	3¼ quarts	One 2- or 3-gallon	3 Tbsp.	½ tsp. New Black; ½ tsp. Khaki	1 Tbsp.

tsp. = teaspoon; Tbsp. = tablespoon

Circle Quilt pillow in peach and green

Circle Quilt throw in
peach and green

PEACH AND GREEN—THROW

FABRIC		WATER	BUCKETS	SALT	DYE	SODA ASH
PEACH 5-STEP GRADATION	5 pieces 1 yard each	2 quarts each	Five 1-gallon	2 Tbsp.* each	Dye solution = 1¼ tsp.* Light Red, 1½ tsp. Deep Yellow, and ¼ tsp. Khaki dissolved in ¼ cup water	2 tsp. each
GREEN	¾ yard	1½ quarts	One 1-gallon	1½ Tbsp.	½ + ⅛ tsp. Cerulean Blue; ¼ + ⅛ + 1/16 tsp. Lemon Yellow	1½ tsp.
GRAY BACKGROUND	2½ yards	5 quarts	One 2- or 3-gallon	5 Tbsp.	3½ tsp. New Black; 1⅛ tsp. Khaki	5 tsp.
GRAY BACKING	2 yards	4 quarts	One 2- or 3-gallon	4 Tbsp.	2¾ tsp. New Black; 1 tsp. Khaki	4 tsp.
GREEN BACKING AND BINDING	2 yards	4 quarts	One 2- or 3-gallon	4 Tbsp.	1 tsp. Cerulean Blue; ¾ tsp. Lemon Yellow	4 tsp.

* tsp. = teaspoon; Tbsp. = tablespoon

PEACH AND GREEN—QUEEN SIZE

FABRIC		WATER	BUCKETS	SALT	DYE	SODA ASH
PEACH 5-STEP GRADATION	5 pieces 1¾ yards each	3½ quarts each	Five 2- or 3-gallon	4 Tbsp.* each	Dye solution = 2 tsp.* Light Red, 2½ tsp. Deep Yellow, and ½ tsp. Khaki dissolved in ¼ cup water	4 tsp. each
GREEN	1¼ yards	2¾ quarts	One 1-gallon	2½ Tbsp.	½ + ¼ + ⅛ tsp. Cerulean Blue; ½ + 1/16 tsp. Lemon Yellow	1 Tbsp.
GRAY	4 yards	9 quarts	One 5-gallon	½ cup	5½ tsp. New Black; 1¾ tsp. Khaki	2½ Tbsp.
PEACH BORDER	1 yard	2 quarts	One 1-gallon	2 Tbsp.	¼ tsp. Light Red; ¼ + ⅛ tsp. Deep Yellow; 1/16 tsp. Khaki	2 tsp.
GREEN BACKING	2½ yards	5 quarts	One 2- or 3-gallon	5 Tbsp.	1 tsp. Cerulean Blue; ¾ tsp. Lemon Yellow	5 tsp.
PEACH BACKING AND BINDING	2½ yards	5 quarts	One 2- or 3-gallon	5 Tbsp.	⅛ + 1/16 tsp. Light Red; ¼ tsp. Deep Yellow; 1/32 tsp. Khaki	5 tsp.
GRAY BACKING	2½ yards	5 quarts	One 2- or 3-gallon	5 Tbsp.	3½ tsp. New Black; 1⅛ tsp. Khaki	5 tsp.

* tsp. = teaspoon; Tbsp. = tablespoon

Circle Quilt throw in peach and green

DYE PROCEDURES

Five-Step Gradations

1. Soak the 5 pieces of fabric in warm water.

2. Line up 5 plastic containers that will hold enough water for the recipe with room for fabric and stirring. Label each container with a piece of tape and number the containers 1 through 5. Add the required amount of water to each container.

3. Add the required amount of salt to each container and stir well.

4. *For the blue gradation only:* In a small dry container, measure the listed amount of Cerulean Blue dye powder and dissolve it using 5 tablespoons warm water. Add 1 tablespoon of the Cerulean Blue dye solution to each of the 5 containers.

5. In a separate small dry container, measure the amount of dye powder listed for the dye solution to make either the black or the peach. Dissolve the dye powder using ¼ cup warm water and stir it well. This is your working dye solution.

6. Make the gradation dye baths using either the peach or the black working dye solution mixed in Step 5.

DYE BATH #5:

- Add ⅛ cup working dye solution to container/dye bath #5.

DYE BATH #4:

- Add ⅛ cup water to the remaining working dye solution and stir well to make a new working dye solution.

- Add ⅛ cup of the new working dye solution to container/dye bath #4.

DYE BATH #3:

- Add ⅛ cup water to the remaining working dye solution and stir well to make a new working dye solution.

- Add ⅛ cup of the new working dye solution to container/dye bath #3.

DYE BATH #2:

- Add ⅛ cup water to the remaining working dye solution and stir well to make a new working dye solution.

- Add ⅛ cup of the new working dye solution to container/dye bath #2.

DYE BATH #1

For the blue gradation:

- Don't add any black dye to container/dye bath #1.

- Discard the last ⅛ cup of working dye solution.

For the peach:

- Add ⅛ cup water to the working dye solution and stir well.

- Add ⅛ cup of the new working dye solution to container/dye bath #1.

- Discard the last ⅛ cup of dye solution.

7. Stir each dye bath again. Add a piece of damp fabric to each dye bath and stir well for 10 minutes.

8. Add the required amount of soda ash to each dye bath and stir well.

9. Stir the dye baths well for 30 minutes.

10. Wash out the fabric (page 23). Dry and iron the dyed fabric. Label the fabrics with the dye bath numbers.

Remaining Fabrics

The rest of the fabrics for both versions are dyed following the basic dyeing instructions in How to Dye Fabric (page 20). Refer to the charts above for the quantities of water, salt, soda ash, and dye powder.

CUTTING INSTRUCTIONS

Copy *Circle Quilt* patterns A and B (pages 68 and 69) at 200%. Copy pattern C (page 69) at 100%. Use your favorite method to prepare templates for cutting the quilt pieces as indicated. The first color given in the instructions is for the blue and orange quilt, and the second color (in parentheses) is for the peach and green quilt.

- From white (gray):

    Cut the fabric into the given number of strips 10½″ × width of fabric. Trace template A onto each strip, rotating the template as you go to fit as many on the strip as possible.

    FOR PILLOW: Cut 1 strip 10½″ × width of fabric; trace and cut 4 pieces with template A.

    FOR THROW: Cut 6 strips 10½″ × width of fabric; trace and cut 36 pieces with template A.

    FOR QUEEN SIZE: Cut 12 strips 10½″ × width of fabric; trace and cut 72 pieces with template A.

- From blue gradations #1, #2, #3, and #5 (peach gradations #1, #2, #3, and #5):

    Cut each of the #1, #2, #3, and #5 gradation fabrics into the given number of strips 9¾″ × width of fabric. Trace template B onto each strip, rotating the template to fit as many on the strip as possible.

    FOR PILLOW: Cut 1 strip 9¾″ × width of fabric; trace and cut 1 piece from each color with template B.

    FOR THROW: Cut 2 strips 9¾″ × width of fabric; trace and cut 9 from each color with template B.

    FOR QUEEN SIZE: Cut 5 strips 9¾″ × width of fabric; trace and cut 18 from each color with template B.

- From orange and blue gradation #4 (green and peach gradation #4):

    Cut each of the orange and blue #4 (green and peach #4) fabrics into the given number of strips 4½″ × width of fabric. Trace template C onto each strip, rotating the template to fit as many on the strip as possible.

    FOR PILLOW:

    Cut 1 orange (green) strip 4½″ × width of fabric; trace and cut 3 pieces with template C.

    Cut 1 blue #4 (peach #4) strip 4½″ × width of fabric; trace and cut 1 piece with template C.

    FOR THROW:

    Cut 4 orange (green) strips 4½″ × width of fabric; trace and cut 27 pieces with template C.

    Cut 2 blue #4 (peach #4) strips 4½″ × width of fabric; trace and cut 9 pieces with template C.

    FOR QUEEN-SIZE QUILT:

    Cut 7 orange (green) strips 4½″ × width of fabric; trace and cut 54 pieces with template C.

    Cut 3 blue #4 (peach #4) strips 4½″ × width of fabric; trace and cut 18 pieces with template C.

CONSTRUCTION

Seam allowances are ¼˝.

Circle Block Assembly

1. Fold all the A, B, and C pieces in half and mark the center of each curve with a pin. (All the B pieces will have 2 pins, 1 on each curve.)

2. To make 1 block, pair up the blue #5 (peach #5) B piece with the blue #4 (peach #4) C piece. With right sides together, match up the centers on the B and C pieces, pin the center and the ends, and carefully sew the pieces together, maintaining a consistent ¼˝ seam allowance.

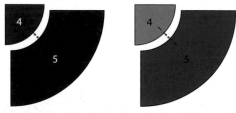

Match center pins of piece B and piece C.

3. Repeat Step 2, matching the blue #1, blue #2, and blue #3 B pieces with orange C pieces (peach #1, peach #2, and peach #3 B pieces with green C pieces).

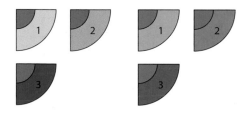

4. Press the seams toward piece C. The curves here are gentle enough that they don't need to be clipped, but if the seams aren't lying flat, carefully clip the seams or use pinking shears to trim the seam allowance before pressing the seams.

5. Pair up a white (gray) A piece with a blue (peach) B/C unit. With right sides together, match up the centers on piece A and unit B/C, pin the centers and the ends, and carefully sew the pieces together, maintaining a consistent ¼˝ seam allowance.

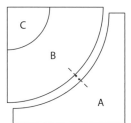

Match center pins of piece A and unit B/C.

6. Press the seams toward piece B. Each quarter-circle block should measure 10½˝ × 10½˝. Square up and trim the blocks if necessary.

7. Using the dye bath numbers for the fabrics in the diagrams, follow the diagram for color order. Sew 4 quarter-circle blocks together, matching the seams, to make a full block. There are 2 different block assemblies for the blue and orange blocks. The peach and green blocks are all sewn the same. Make the number of blocks indicated for the quilt you are making. Press the seams open. If you are making either of the queen-size quilts, you will have 8 extra quarter-circle blocks that you will use in the quilt assembly.

Blue and orange block 1: Make 1 for pillow, make 9 for throw, and make 8 for queen size.

Blue and orange block 2: Make 8 for queen size.

Peach and green block: Make 1 for pillow, make 9 for throw, and make 16 for queen size.

8. Square and trim the blocks to 20½″ × 20½″.

Quilt Assembly

PILLOW

Refer to the pillow photos (pages 55 and 58).

1. For the blue and orange pillow, cut the white backing fabric into 2 pieces 20½″ × 28″ and 1 piece 24″ × 24″. For the peach and green pillow, cut the gray backing fabric into 2 pieces 20½″ × 28″ and 1 piece 24″ × 24″.

2. Layer the Circle block with the batting and 24″ × 24″ piece of backing. Quilt; then trim to 20½″ × 20½″. Refer to Layering (page 131).

3. Fold each 20½″ × 28″ piece of backing in half and press the crease to make 2 pieces that are each 20½″ × 14″.

4. Topstitch the pressed edges with matching thread.

5. Place the Circle block wrong side down on the table. Line up the raw edges of the 2 pieces 20½″ × 14″ with the raw edges of the Circle block on the wrong side, so the pressed and stitched edges are in the middle of the block.

6. Pin in place and sew around the edge of the entire block with a scant ¼″ seam. Clip the corners.

7. Turn the pillow right side out and push the corners of the pillow out to make a nice square. Topstitch along the edge of the pillow, using matching thread.

8. Insert the pillow form.

THROW AND QUEEN-SIZE QUILT

*Refer to the quilt photos (pages 57 and 61)
and to the quilt assembly diagrams, at right.*

1. Refer to the quilt diagram for the quilt
that you are making and arrange the blocks as
shown. If you are making either of the queen-
size quilts, arrange the large blocks and use
the remaining 8 quarter-circle blocks in the
bottom row as shown.

2. Sew together the blocks in rows,
matching the seams. Press the seams open.

3. Sew together the rows. Press the
seams open.

Borders

For the queen size:

1. Cut the orange (peach) border fabric into
9 strips 3˝ × width of fabric.

2. Sew the strips together as if you were
making binding strips (page 132) to make
2 strips 90½˝ and 2 strips 85½˝ long.

3. Sew the 90½˝-long strips to the sides and
press the seams toward the border strips.

4. Sew the 85½˝-long strips to the top
and bottom. Press the seams toward the
border strips.

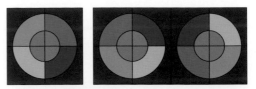
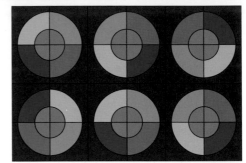

Quilt assembly diagram for throw

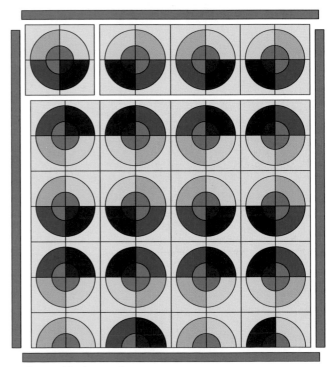

Quilt assembly diagram for queen size

Pieced Backing

THROW

1. Iron the 2 pieces of fabric listed in the materials section for the backing.

2. Trim off the selvages of each piece of fabric and square up the ends, so you have clean lines for piecing.

3. Cut the orange (green) piece into 2 pieces 14″ × 72″ and 28″ × 72″. Set aside the smaller piece to use for the binding.

4. Sew the remaining orange (green) piece and the white (gray) piece together along the trimmed long edge to make 1 large piece approximately 72″ × 70″. Press the seam open.

5. Trim the backing to 66″ × 66″.

QUEEN-SIZE QUILT

1. Iron the 3 pieces of fabric listed in the materials section for the backing.

2. Trim off the selvages of each piece of fabric and square up the ends, so you have clean lines for piecing.

3. Cut the blue (peach) fabric into 2 pieces 20″ × 90″. Set 1 piece aside to use for binding.

4. Sew the 3 pieces together with the blue (peach) in the middle. Press the seams open. Trim the backing to 96″ × 102″.

FINISHING

Refer to Quiltmaking Basics: Finishing (page 130) to layer, quilt, and bind the quilt.

NOTE

Use the extra fabric left from the quilt backing to bind the throw and queen-size quilt.

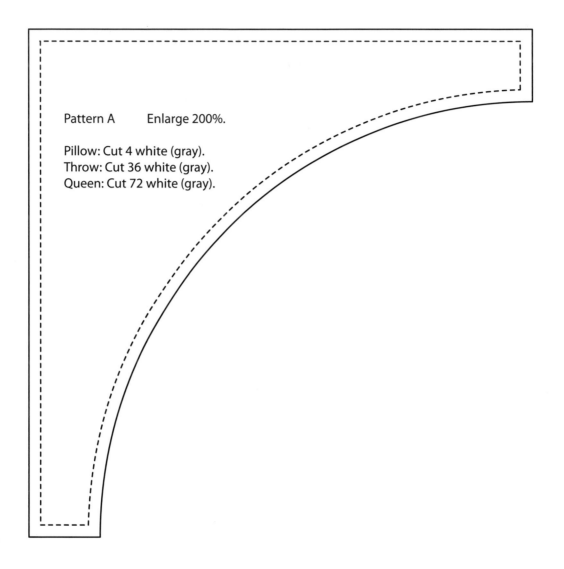

Pattern A   Enlarge 200%.

Pillow: Cut 4 white (gray).
Throw: Cut 36 white (gray).
Queen: Cut 72 white (gray).

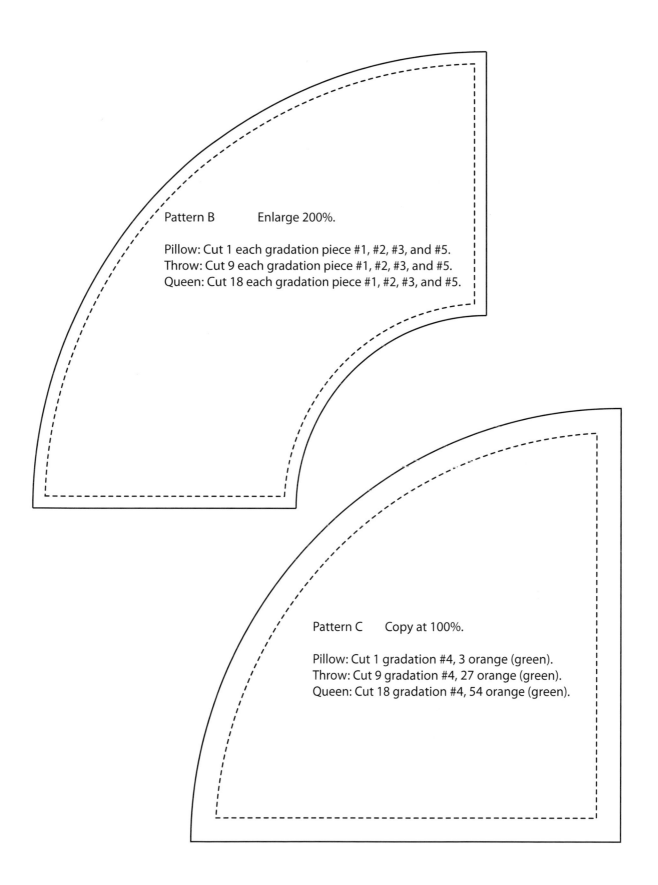

Pattern B   Enlarge 200%.

Pillow: Cut 1 each gradation piece #1, #2, #3, and #5.
Throw: Cut 9 each gradation piece #1, #2, #3, and #5.
Queen: Cut 18 each gradation piece #1, #2, #3, and #5.

Pattern C   Copy at 100%.

Pillow: Cut 1 gradation #4, 3 orange (green).
Throw: Cut 9 gradation #4, 27 orange (green).
Queen: Cut 18 gradation #4, 54 orange (green).

PINEAPPLE LOG CABIN QUILT

FINISHED BLOCK: 16″ × 16″

FINISHED QUILT: 16″ × 16″ for pillow, 16″ × 64″ for table runner, 64″ × 64″ for throw

The Pineapple Log Cabin is one of my favorite quilt patterns. There are endless possible variations, and the look of a quilt can change immensely just by changing the way color and value are used in the pattern. As in a regular Log Cabin, the Pineapple Log Cabin is worked from the center and is made from strips of fabric that are trimmed after sewing. However, instead of working around a block with four sides, the Pineapple Log Cabin has eight sides until the very last row turns it into a square. This quilt, more than any other in the book, requires careful work, attention to detail, and a really consistent scant ¼″ seam. And just so you know, there are a lot of seams to sew, so it uses a lot of thread. A lot.

I read somewhere that pineapples were a symbol of friendship and hospitality in early America. Both versions of this quilt are bright and inviting and would make great gifts. The yellow version is perfect for summer, reminiscent of the frozen pineapple treat Dole Whip. The red version reminds me of poinsettias, and I will be using mine as a Christmas decoration.

MATERIALS AND EQUIPMENT

Yardage is based on 44″-wide fabric.

	PILLOW	TABLE RUNNER	THROW
WHITE (UNDYED) FABRIC	2½ yards*	5 yards*	14¾ yards*
BATTING	20″ × 20″	20″ × 68″	70″ × 70″
PILLOW FORM	16″ × 16″		
BUCKETS	Six 1-quart	Six 1-gallon and one 1-quart	Five 1-gallon, one 1-quart, and one 5-gallon

* Note: If you want to dye fabric for only part of the quilt, refer to the project charts (pages 73, 74, 76, and 78) for the amount of fabric needed for each part.

Pineapple Log Cabin Quilt
throw and pillow in yellow

COLOR RECIPES

The green center squares in the red version are dyed as described in How to Dye Fabric (page 20).

Both versions of this quilt also use a gradation. The setup for each dye bath is the same as for a non-gradation, but the difference is in how the dye is measured and added to the dye bath.

NOTE

You will be making dye solutions for the gradations, and there is also a special procedure for the light blue center squares in the yellow version. Read through the instructions for making the light blue dye solution (below) and all the gradation instructions (page 79) before you set up your dye baths.

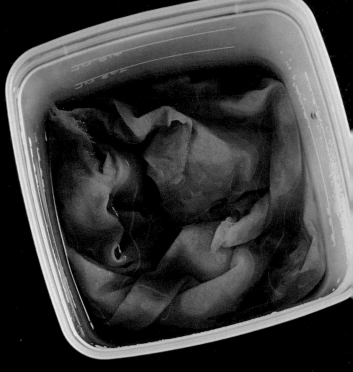

Light Blue Dye Solution

The light blue in the yellow version is so light and used in such small quantities that it is difficult to measure accurately using dry dye powder. To make this process easier, a dye solution is used. A dye solution is simply a specific amount of dye dissolved in a specific quantity of water.

For the yellow pillow and the yellow table runner, set up 3 small plastic containers each with 2 table-spoons water. Measure and dissolve ¼ teaspoon Cerulean Blue into the first cup, ¼ teaspoon New Black into the second cup, and ¼ teaspoon Light Red into the third cup.

For the yellow throw, set up 3 small plastic containers each with 6 tablespoons water. Measure and dissolve ¾ teaspoon Cerulean Blue in the first cup, ¾ teaspoon New Black in the second cup, and ¾ teaspoon Light Red in the third cup.

IMPORTANT FOR LIGHT BLUE

In the following dye recipe chart, you will measure from these dye solutions instead of the dry dye powder for the light blue fabric. These charts also tell you how to divide the fabric for the various dye baths.

Note: You will be using the leftover yellow or red fabric from the pillow, table runner, and throw as binding.

YELLOW−PILLOW

FABRIC		WATER	BUCKETS	SALT	DYE	SODA ASH
YELLOW 5-STEP GRADATION	5 fat eighths*	1 cup each	Five 1-quart	¾ tsp.** each	Dye solution for gradation: ¼ + ¹⁄₁₆ tsp. Deep Yellow and ¹⁄₃₂ tsp. Cerulean Blue dissolved in ¼ cup water	¼ tsp. each
LIGHT BLUE	¼ yard	2¼ cups	One 1-quart	1½ tsp.	1 tsp. Cerulean Blue solution; ¹⁄₁₆ tsp. New Black solution; ¹⁄₁₆ tsp. Light Red solution	½ tsp.
WHITE (UNDYED)	¼ yard					
WHITE (UNDYED) PILLOW BACK	1 yard					

* Fat eighth = 10″ × 18″
** tsp. = teaspoon

Pineapple Log Cabin Quilt
pillow in yellow

YELLOW—TABLE RUNNER

FABRIC		WATER	BUCKETS	SALT	DYE	SODA ASH
YELLOW 5-STEP GRA-DATION	5 pieces ½ yard each	1 quart each	Five 1-gallon	1 Tbsp.** each	Dye solution for gradation: 1 + ¼ + ⅛ tsp.** Deep Yellow and ⅛ + 1/32 tsp. Cerulean Blue dissolved in ¼ cup water	1 tsp. each
LIGHT BLUE	1 fat eighth*	1 cup	One 1-quart	¾ tsp.	½ tsp. Cerulean Blue solution; 1/32 tsp. New Black solution; 1/32 tsp. Light Red solution	¼ tsp.
WHITE (UNDYED)	1 yard					
LIGHT BLUE BACKING	1 yard	2 quarts	One 1-gallon	2 Tbsp.	3¼ tsp. Cerulean Blue solution; ¼ + ⅛ tsp. New Black solution; ¼ + ⅛ tsp. Light Red solution	2 Tbsp.

Fat eighth = 10″ × 18″

*** tsp. = teaspoon; Tbsp. = tablespoon*

YELLOW—THROW

FABRIC		WATER	BUCKETS	SALT	DYE	SODA ASH
YELLOW 5-STEP GRADATION	5 pieces 1¼ yards each	2½ quarts each	Five 1-gallon	2½ Tbsp.* each	Dye solution for gradation: 3¼ tsp.* Deep Yellow and ¼ + ⅛ tsp. Cerulean Blue dissolved in ¼ cup water	2½ tsp. each
LIGHT BLUE	⅓ yard	2¼ cups	One 1-quart	1½ tsp.	1 tsp. Cerulean Blue solution; 1/16 tsp. New Black solution; 1/16 tsp. Light Red solution	½ tsp.
WHITE (UNDYED)	4 yards					
LIGHT BLUE BACKING	4 yards	9 quarts	One 5-gallon	½ cup	4½ Tbsp. Cerulean Blue solution; ¾ tsp. New Black solution; ¾ tsp. Light Red solution	2½ Tbsp.

** tsp. = teaspoon; Tbsp. = tablespoon*

Pineapple Log Cabin Quilt throw in yellow

RED—PILLOW

FABRIC		WATER	BUCKETS	SALT	DYE	SODA ASH
RED 5-STEP GRADATION	5 fat eighths*	1 cup each	Five 1-quart	¾ tsp.** each	Dye solution for gradation: ½ + ¹⁄₁₆ tsp. Light Red and ⅛ + ¹⁄₁₆ tsp. Deep Yellow dissolved in ¼ cup water	¼ tsp. each
GREEN	¼ yard	2¼ cups	One 1-quart	1½ tsp.	¼ tsp. Lemon Yellow; ¼ tsp. Cerulean Blue	½ tsp.
WHITE (UNDYED)	¼ yard					
WHITE (UNDYED) PILLOW BACK	1 yard					

Fat eighth = 10″ × 18″
*** tsp. = teaspoon*

RED—THROW

FABRIC		WATER	BUCKETS	SALT	DYE	SODA ASH
RED 5-STEP GRADATION	5 pieces 1¼ yards each	2½ quarts each	Five 1-gallon	3 Tbsp.* each	Dye solution for gradation: 5½ tsp* Light Red and 2 tsp. Deep Yellow dissolved in ¼ cup water	3 tsp. each
GREEN	1¼ yards	2½ quarts	One 1-gallon	3 Tbsp.	1½ tsp. Lemon Yellow; 1½ tsp. Cerulean Blue	3 tsp.
WHITE (UNDYED)	3 yards					
GREEN BACKING	4 yards	9 quarts	One 5-gallon	½ cup	4½ tsp. Lemon Yellow; 4½ tsp. Cerulean Blue	2½ Tbsp.

tsp. = teaspoon; Tbsp. = tablespoon

Pineapple Log Cabin Quilt
table runner in red

RED—TABLE RUNNER

FABRIC		WATER	BUCKETS	SALT	DYE	SODA ASH
RED 5-STEP GRADATION	5 pieces ½ yard each	1 quart each	Five 1-gallon	1 Tbsp.* each	Dye solution for gradation: 2¼ tsp.* Light Red and ¾ tsp. Deep Yellow dissolved in ¼ cup water	1 tsp. each
GREEN	½ yard	1 quart	One 1-gallon	1 Tbsp.	½ tsp. Lemon Yellow; ½ tsp. Cerulean Blue	1 tsp.
WHITE (UNDYED)	1 yard					
GREEN BACKING	1 yard	2 quarts	One 1-gallon	2 Tbsp.	1 tsp. Lemon Yellow; 1 tsp. Cerulean Blue	2 tsp.

* tsp. = teaspoon; Tbsp. = tablespoon

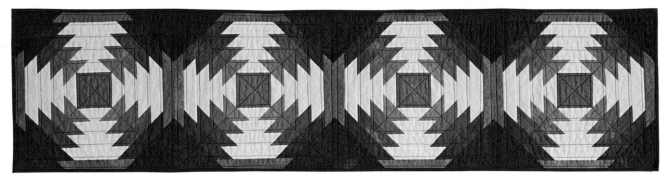

Pineapple Log Cabin Quilt table runner in red

DYE PROCEDURE FOR FIVE-STEP GRADATIONS

1. Soak the 5 pieces of fabric in warm water.

2. Line up 5 plastic containers that will hold enough water for the recipe with room for fabric and stirring. Label each container with a piece of tape and number the containers 1 through 5. Add the required amount of water to each container.

3. Add the required amount of salt to each container and stir well.

4. Mix up the dye solution for the gradation as shown in the charts above. Stir well to make sure the dye powder is dissolved.

5. Make the 5 gradation dye baths using either the red or the yellow working dye solution mixed in Step 4.

6. Stir each dye bath again. Add a piece of damp fabric to each dye bath and stir well for 10 minutes.

7. Add the required amount of soda ash to each dye bath and stir well.

8. Stir the dye baths well for 30 minutes.

9. Wash out the fabric (page 23).

10. Dry and iron the dyed fabric. Label each fabric with the dye bath number.

DYE BATH #5:

- Starting with container/dye bath #5, add ⅛ cup working dye solution and stir well.

DYE BATH #4:

- Add ⅛ cup water to the remaining working dye solution and stir well to make new working dye solution.

- Add ⅛ cup of the new working dye solution to container/dye bath #4.

DYE BATH #3:

- Add ⅛ cup water to the remaining working dye solution and stir well to make new working dye solution.

- Add ⅛ cup of the new working dye solution to container/dye bath #3.

DYE BATH #2:

- Add ⅛ cup water to the remaining working dye solution and stir well to make new working dye solution.

- Add ⅛ cup of the new working dye solution to container/dye bath #2.

DYE BATH #1:

- Add ⅛ cup water to the remaining working dye solution and stir well to make new working dye solution.

- Add ⅛ cup of the new working dye solution to container/dye bath #1.

- Discard the last ⅛ cup of working dye solution.

CUTTING INSTRUCTIONS FOR YELLOW VERSIONS

Important: Don't cut all the yellow fabric into strips. You will be using the extra for the binding.

- **From white:**

  Cut the entire piece into strips 1¾″ × width of fabric.

- **From light blue:**

  FOR PILLOW: Cut 1 square 4″ × 4″.

  FOR TABLE RUNNER: Cut 4 squares 4″ × 4″.

  FOR THROW: Cut 16 squares 4″ × 4″.

- **From yellow gradation #5:**

  FOR PILLOW: Cut 2 squares 6½″ × 6½″.

  FOR TABLE RUNNER: Cut 8 squares 6½″ × 6½″.

  FOR THROW: Cut 32 squares 6½″ × 6½″.

- **From yellow gradations #1, #2, #3, and #4:**

  FOR ALL SIZES: Cut the fabric into strips 1¾″ × width of fabric, except for the fat eighths. Cut those strips 1¾″ × 18″. You will need less of the lighter colors and more of the darker colors. The strips will be cut down into smaller lengths when you start piecing them. I recommend the following:

  FOR PILLOW AND TABLE RUNNER: Start by cutting about half of the fabric into strips. It is easy to cut more strips as you need them.

  FOR THROW: Start by cutting 3 strips of gradation #1, 4 strips of gradation #2, 4 strips of gradation #3, and 5 strips of gradation #4. Depending on how much overlap you leave when piecing, you may cut more as needed.

CONSTRUCTION

Seam allowances are ¼″.

Pineapple Block Assembly

For each pillow, make 1 block. For each table runner, make 4 blocks. For each throw, make 16 blocks. The first color given is for the yellow versions, and the second color (in parentheses) is for the red versions. The white strips are the same in both the yellow and the red projects, unless noted.

1. From a 1¾″ white strip, cut 2 pieces 1¾″ × 4½″ and 2 pieces 1¾″ × 8½″.

2. Sew a white 4½″ strip to the top and another to the bottom of a blue (green) 4″ × 4″ square. Press the seams toward the white strips and trim the edges even with the square.

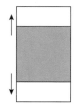

Sew white strips to center square.

3. Sew white 8½″ strips to the sides as shown. Press the seams toward the white strips. Trim the block to 6½″ × 6½″ square, keeping the blue (green) square centered.

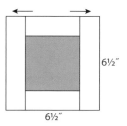

Sew white strips to sides and trim.

4. Fold the block in half with right sides together, matching the seams. Finger-press a crease into the top and bottom of the white strips. Repeat to finger-press a crease into the left and right sides. Measure ½″ on each side of the 4 creases and make a tiny mark with a pencil.

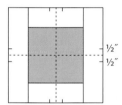

Finger-press centers and mark 1/2″ on each side of creases.

5. Place a strip of the lightest yellow #1 (red #1) diagonally across the block and cut it so the length is about ½″ longer than the distance between the pencil marks. Cut 4 (pillow), 16 (table runner), or 64 (throw) pieces the same length.

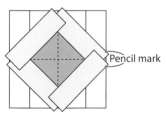

Strips laid on top of block, not yet sewn

CUTTING INSTRUCTIONS FOR RED VERSIONS

Important: Don't cut all the red fabric into strips. You will use the leftover fabric for the binding.

- From white:

  Cut the entire piece into strips 1¾″ × width of fabric.

- From green:

  FOR PILLOW: Cut 1 square 4″ × 4″. Cut the remaining green into strips 1¾″ × width of fabric.

  FOR TABLE RUNNER: Cut 4 squares 4″ × 4″. Cut the remaining green into strips 1¾″ × width of fabric.

  FOR THROW: Cut 16 squares 4″ × 4″. Cut the remaining green into strips 1¾″ × width of fabric.

- From red gradation #5:

  FOR PILLOW: Cut 2 squares 6½″ × 6½″.

  FOR TABLE RUNNER: Cut 8 squares 6½″ × 6½″.

  FOR THROW: Cut 32 squares 6½″ × 6½″.

- From red gradations #1, #2, #3, and #4:

  FOR ALL SIZES: Cut the fabric into strips 1¾″ × width of fabric, except for the fat eighths. Cut those strips 1¾″ × 18″. You will need less of the lighter colors and more of the darker colors. The strips will be cut down into smaller lengths once you start piecing them. I recommend the following:

  FOR PILLOW AND TABLE RUNNER: Start by cutting about half the fabric into strips. It is easy to cut more strips as you need them.

  FOR THROW: Start by cutting 3 strips of gradation #1, 4 strips of gradation #2, 4 strips of gradation #3, and 5 strips of gradation #4. Depending on how much overlap you leave when piecing, you may cut more as needed.

6. With right sides together, lay a strip across a corner and align the edge of the strip with the pencil marks. Use a ¼″ seam to sew the strip in place. Trim off the white corner as shown. Continue to sew a strip on each corner. For this first round of gradation strips, it is easiest to sew on opposite sides first, finger-press them open, and then sew on the other sides.

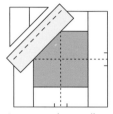

Sew strips diagonally.

7. Press the seams toward the piece you just sewed on. Trim the excess gradation strips using the center square to help square up the block.

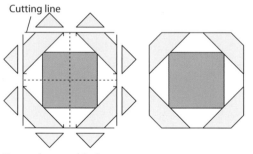

Trim and square block.

8. Place a strip of white along the top edge of the block, parallel to the center square. Cut the strip about 1″ longer than the length of the side. Cut 4 (pillow), 16 (table runner), or 64 (throw) pieces of white the same length.

9. Sew the pieces of white to each side of the block. Press the seams toward the outside of the block.

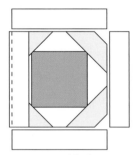

Sew strips to block.

10. Trim off the excess white strips as shown.

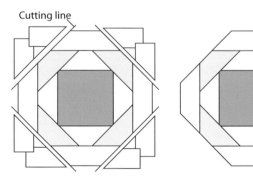

Sew strips to block and trim.

11. Continue alternating rows of gradation fabrics with rows of white fabric, working from light to dark with the gradations. The process is the same for each round: sew on the next row of color on each side, press the seams outward, and trim off the excess. Use the previous rows and the marks on your ruler to help you keep the blocks square. Cut additional strips as needed to complete the rounds on the block. (*Note: For the red version, use green strips in place of white for the last row.*)

Each block will have 4 rows of gradation fabric and 5 rows of white (4 white and 1 green for the red version).

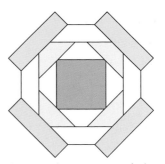

Continue alternating rows of white and gradations.

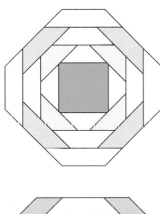

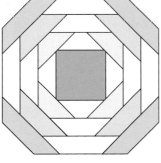

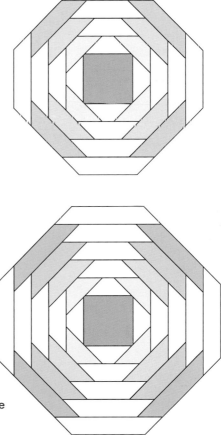

TIP

When making the table runner or throw, it is more efficient to do all of one step at a time on every block, rather than making one block at a time.

12. Cut each 6½″ × 6½″ darkest gradation square in half diagonally to make 2 triangles. With right sides together, pin a triangle to each corner of the Pineapple Log Cabin block, overlapping the ends of the triangles ¼″. Then sew the triangles in place with a ¼″ seam.

Add half-square triangles to corners of blocks.

13. Press the seams toward the triangles and trim the block to 16½″ × 16½″.

Finished block

14. Repeat these steps to make the blocks needed for your project.

Quilt Assembly

PILLOW

Refer to the pillow photo (page 73).

1. Cut the backing fabric into 2 pieces 16½″ × 20″ and 1 piece 20″ × 20″.

2. Layer the Pineapple Log Cabin block with the batting and 20″ × 20″ piece of backing. Baste, quilt, and then trim to 16½″ × 16½″. Refer to Layering (page 131).

3. Fold each 16½″ × 20″ piece of backing in half and press the crease to make 2 pieces that are each 16½″ × 10″.

4. Topstitch the pressed edges with matching thread.

5. Place the Pineapple Log Cabin block facedown on the table. Line up the raw edges of the 2 pieces 16½″ × 10″ with the raw edges of the Pineapple Log Cabin block so the pressed and top-stitched edges are in the middle of the block.

6. Pin in place and baste (sew with a longer stitch length) around the edge of the entire block with a scant ¼″ seam.

7. Refer to Binding (page 132) to bind the pillow as you would a quilt, using the leftover yellow (red) fabric.

8. Insert the pillow form.

TABLE RUNNER

Refer to the table runner photo (page 78).

1. Arrange the 4 Pineapple Log Cabin blocks together in a long strip. It is helpful to try out different block placements before sewing by lining up the blocks and rotating them, if necessary, to get the best match of the last row of white or green. Sew the blocks together and press the seams open.

2. Cut the backing fabric in half, so that you have 2 pieces 20″ × 36″. Trim them, if necessary, and sew them together to make 1 long piece that is 20″ × 72″. Press the seam open. Trim the backing to 20″ × 68″.

Refer to the quilt photo (page 75).

1. Arrange the 16 Pineapple Log Cabin blocks in 4 rows of 4 blocks each. It is helpful to try out different block placements by placing the blocks on the floor or a design wall and matching them up one at a time, rotating them to get the best match of the last row of white (green).

2. Sew together the blocks into rows, and then sew together the rows. Press the seams open.

3. Cut the backing fabric in half, so that you have 2 pieces approximately 40″ × 72″. Trim off the selvages and square up the ends. Sew the pieces together along the 72″ sides to make 1 large piece that is approximately 79″ × 72″. Press the seam open. Trim the backing to 70″ × 70″.

Binding

For all the sizes, cut the remaining yellow (red) gradation pieces into strips 2½″ × width of fabric. Sew the strips together as you normally would for binding (page 132). You can choose to continue the gradation effect by sewing the strips together in order, or mix up the order for a patchwork effect.

FINISHING

Refer to Quiltmaking Basics: Finishing (page 130) to layer, quilt, and bind the table runner or throw.

Pineapple Log Cabin Quilt
pillow in yellow

KNIT QUILT

FINISHED BLOCK: 5″ × 5″ for crib size, 8″ × 8″ for twin size
FINISHED QUILT: 40″ × 50″ for crib size, 64″ × 80″ for twin size

Though made entirely of woven cotton fabric, the *Knit Quilt* combines two of my most favorite things: quilting and knitting. I find it funny that the simplest block ever, the Half-Square Triangle, can look just like a knit stitch graphed out for intarsia or Fair Isle knitting. I've never been very good at either of those—too many floats and twisting yarns and tension issues. So here I can enjoy the best of both worlds!

These two quilts use a slightly different dye method that I use when I want beautiful mottled color. The technique uses less water and dye and doesn't need any stirring. The results can sometimes be surprising, but that is part of the fun of dyeing fabric. The crib-size quilt works great as a wallhanging, too.

MATERIALS AND EQUIPMENT

Yardage is based on 44″-wide fabric.

	CRIB SIZE	TWIN SIZE
WHITE (UNDYED) FABRIC	7⅝ yards*	15½ yards*
QUILT BATTING	46″ × 56″	70″ × 86″
BUCKETS—FOR GREEN AND GRAY VERSION	Ten 1-quart and one 1-gallon	Ten 1-quart and three 1-gallon
BUCKETS—FOR PURPLE AND GREEN VERSION	Eight 1-quart and one 1-gallon	Eight 1-quart and three 1-gallon

* Note: If you want to dye fabric for only part of the quilt, refer to the project charts (pages 90 and 93) for the amount of fabric needed for each part.

Crib-size *Knit Quilt* in green and gray

PREPARING THE FABRIC FOR DYEING

Divide the fabric according to the following charts.

GREEN AND GRAY QUILT

	CRIB SIZE	TWIN SIZE
GRADATIONS	10 pieces ½ yard each	10 pieces ¾ yard each
WHITE (UNDYED)	¾ yard	1½ yards
BACKING	1⅝ yards*	6 yards

PURPLE WITH GREEN QUILT

	CRIB SIZE	TWIN SIZE
GRADATIONS	7 pieces ½ yard each	7 pieces 1 yard each
GREEN	½ yard	¾ yard
WHITE (UNDYED)	¾ yard	1½ yards
BACKING	1⅝ yards*	6 yards

Fabric must be at least 44″ wide.

COLOR RECIPES AND DYEING PROCESS

Quilt Top

The dyeing process for these quilts is different than for the other quilts in the book. Read through the instructions before setting up your dye baths and refer to How to Dye Fabric (page 20) as needed. There is no salt in these recipes because the goal is to create mottled color (salt helps achieve even results, so you don't need it here). Both quilts appear to have two gradations, but each gradation shares black, so the dyeing process is simplified.

1. Put the fabric in a large bucket of warm water to soak while you set up.

2. Mix the dye solutions at right and set them aside.

	DYE SOLUTION 1	DYE SOLUTION 2
GREEN AND GRAY— CRIB	5 tsp.* Deep Yellow and ½ + ⅛ tsp. Cerulean Blue dissolved in 10 Tbsp.* water	2¼ tsp. New Black dissolved in 1½ cups water
GREEN AND GRAY— TWIN	7½ tsp. Deep Yellow and ½ + ¼ + ⅛ tsp. Cerulean Blue dissolved in 10 Tbsp. water	1 Tbsp. New Black dissolved in 1½ cups water
PURPLE WITH GREEN— CRIB	3¼ tsp. Cerulean Blue and ¾ tsp. Light Red dissolved in 1¼ cups water	1½ tsp. New Black dissolved in ½ cup water
PURPLE WITH GREEN— TWIN	4¾ tsp. Cerulean Blue and 1¼ tsp. Light Red dissolved in 1¼ cups water	2¼ tsp. New Black dissolved in ½ cup water

* tsp. = teaspoon; Tbsp. = tablespoon

3. To make the green fabric in the purple with green version, you will need 4 additional dye solutions: Add ¼ cup warm water to each of 4 small plastic containers. Add ½ teaspoon Deep Yellow to the first container, ½ teaspoon Lemon Yellow to the second container, ½ teaspoon Cerulean Blue to the third container, and ½ teaspoon New Black to the fourth container. These amounts apply to both the crib and twin sizes. Stir them well to dissolve and set them aside.

4. Line up 10 quart-size plastic buckets for the green and gray version, or 8 quart-size plastic buckets for the purple and gray version. Label the buckets with the dye bath number.

5. Dissolve the required amount of soda ash in the listed amount of water below and set aside.

SODA ASH

GREEN AND GRAY—CRIB	3½ Tbsp.* soda ash dissolved in 1¼ cups water
GREEN AND GRAY—TWIN	5 Tbsp. soda ash dissolved in 1¼ cups water
PURPLE WITH GREEN—CRIB	2½ Tbsp. soda ash dissolved in 1 cup water
PURPLE WITH GREEN—TWIN	4 Tbsp. soda ash dissolved in 1 cup water

* Tbsp. = tablespoon

6. Gently squeeze out the excess water from the fabric and put 1 piece in each quart-size bucket. It will be a tight fit, but that is what you want for mottled color.

7. Combine the amount of dye solution (mixed in Step 2) from the chart (page 92) with enough water to make 1 cup of dye liquid for each dye bath. As you make a color, pour it over the fabric in the corresponding dye bath bucket and then move on to the next color. There is no need to stir. Quantities listed are for both quilt sizes.

GREEN AND GRAY QUILT

BATH #	1	2	3	4	5	6	7	8	9	10
YELLOW SOLUTION (DYE SOLUTION 1)	2 Tbsp.*	2 Tbsp.	2 Tbsp.	2 Tbsp.	2 Tbsp.	0	0	0	0	0
BLACK SOLUTION (DYE SOLUTION 2)	0	1 tsp.*	1 Tbsp.	2 Tbsp.	¼ cup	½ cup	¼ cup	2 Tbsp.	1 Tbsp.	1 tsp.

tsp. = teaspoon; Tbsp. = tablespoon

PURPLE WITH GREEN QUILT

BATH #	1	2	3	4	5	6	7	8
PURPLE SOLUTION (DYE SOLUTION 1)	½ cup	¼ cup	2 Tbsp.*	1 Tbsp.	1 Tbsp.	1 Tbsp.	1 Tbsp.	0
BLACK SOLUTION (DYE SOLUTION 2)	0	0	0	0	1 Tbsp.	2 Tbsp.	¼ cup	0

Tbsp. = tablespoon

8. Dye bath #8 in the purple with green version is the mottled green fabric. For this you will use the 4 small cups of dye solution from Step 3. Start with the lightest color for best results. Pour some of each color over the fabric in bucket #8. This step is vague because it's fun to experiment and see what happens if you add more or less of a color.

9. Poke the fabrics with a plastic spoon a few times, turn them over with gloved hands, squeeze them with gloved hands, or just leave them alone. The more you poke and squeeze the fabrics, the more even the color will be. If you leave the fabrics alone, there will be very distinct mottling. Do what you want here; there is no right answer.

10. Refer to Activate the Dye (page 22). After a couple of minutes, add 2 tablespoons of the soda ash solution to each dye bath. Continue with the poking and squeezing or with leaving the fabric alone.

11. After 30 minutes, wash out the fabric (page 23).

12. Dry and iron the dyed fabric. Label each fabric with the dye bath number.

Backing and Binding

These recipes will also achieve mottled results, so use the same procedure as above. Larger pieces of fabric might not fit in a quart-size bucket, so find the smallest container you can cram the fabric into and go from there. There will be enough of each gradation fabric left over from the quilt top to make the binding.

GREEN AND GRAY—CRIB SIZE

FABRIC		WATER	DYE	SODA ASH
GRAY BACKING	1⅝ yards	1½ cups	¼ tsp.* New Black	1 Tbsp.* dissolved in 2 Tbsp. water

** tsp. = teaspoon; Tbsp. = tablespoon*

GREEN AND GRAY—TWIN SIZE

FABRIC		WATER	DYE	SODA ASH
GRAY 1 BACKING	2 yards	2 cups	¼ tsp.* New Black	1 Tbsp.* dissolved in 2 Tbsp. water
YELLOW BACKING	2 yards	2 cups	¼ tsp. Deep Yellow; 1/32 tsp. Cerulean Blue	1 Tbsp. dissolved in 2 Tbsp. water
GRAY 2 BACKING	2 yards	2 cups	1 Tbsp. New Black	1 Tbsp. dissolved in 2 Tbsp. water

** tsp. = teaspoon; Tbsp. = tablespoon*

PURPLE WITH GREEN—CRIB SIZE

FABRIC		WATER	DYE	SODA ASH
PURPLE BACKING	1⅝ yards	1½ cups	⅛ tsp.* New Black; ⅛ tsp. Cerulean Blue; 1/32 tsp. Light Red	1 Tbsp.* dissolved in 2 Tbsp. water

** tsp. = teaspoon; Tbsp. = tablespoon*

PURPLE WITH GREEN—TWIN SIZE

FABRIC		WATER	DYE	SODA ASH
GRAY 1 BACKING	2 yards	2 cups	⅛ tsp.* New Black; ⅛ tsp. Cerulean Blue; 1/32 tsp. Light Red	1 Tbsp.* dissolved in 2 Tbsp. water
PURPLE BACKING	2 yards	2 cups	¼ tsp. Cerulean Blue; 1/16 tsp. Light Red	1 Tbsp. dissolved in 2 Tbsp. water

** tsp. = teaspoon; Tbsp. = tablespoon*

Crib-size *Knit Quilt* in green and gray

Modern Color—An Illustrated Guide to Dyeing Fabric for Modern Quilts

Crib-size *Knit Quilt* in purple with green

CUTTING INSTRUCTIONS

All the fabric for the quilt tops will be cut into squares, either 6½″ × 6½″ for the crib size or 9½″ × 9½″ for the twin size. Refer to these charts for the number of squares to cut from each fabric. The numbers in parentheses refer to the dye bath numbers, to identify the fabrics.

GREEN AND GRAY QUILT

FABRIC COLOR	# OF SQUARES TO CUT
Green 1 (#1)	7
Green 2 (#2)	7
Green 3 (#3)	7
Green 4 (#4)	7
Green 5 (#5)	2
Gray 1 (#10)	5
Gray 2 (#9)	7
Gray 3 (#8)	7
Gray 4 (#7)	7
Gray 5 (#6)	7
White	17

PURPLE WITH GREEN QUILT

FABRIC COLOR	# OF SQUARES TO CUT
Purple 1 (#4)	7
Purple 2 (#3)	7
Purple 3 (#2)	7
Purple 4 (#1)	9
Gray 1 (#7)	12
Gray 2 (#6)	7
Gray 3 (#5)	7
Green (#8)	7
White	17

CONSTRUCTION

Seam allowances are ¼″.

Block Assembly

All the squares will be sewn into half-square triangles. Follow the directions for half-square triangles in the *Step Quilt* instructions (page 48). Remember that each pair of squares will make 2 blocks.

You will need the following number of blocks:

GREEN AND GRAY QUILT

COLOR COMBINATION	# OF BLOCKS TO MAKE
Green 1 (#1) and white	4
Green 1 (#1) and gray 1 (#10)	4
Green 1 (#1) and gray 2 (#9)	6
Green 2 (#2) and white	2
Green 2 (#2) and gray 2 (#9)	6
Green 2 (#2) and gray 3 (#8)	6
Green 3 (#3) and white	2
Green 3 (#3) and gray 3 (#8)	6
Green 3 (#3) and gray 4 (#7)	6
Green 4 (#4) and white	2
Green 4 (#4) and gray 4 (#7)	6
Green 4 (#4) and gray 5 (#6)	6
Green 5 (#5) and white	2
Green 5 (#5) and gray 5 (#6)	2
Gray 1 (#10) and white	6
Gray 2 (#9) and white	2
Gray 3 (#8) and white	2
Gray 4 (#7) and white	2
Gray 5 (#6) and white	6
White and white	2

PURPLE WITH GREEN QUILT

COLOR COMBINATION	# OF BLOCKS TO MAKE
Purple 1 (#4) and white	4
Purple 1 (#4) and purple 2 (#3)	6
Purple 1 (#4) and gray 1 (#7)	4
Purple 2 (#3) and purple 3 (#2)	6
Purple 2 (#3) and white	2
Purple 3 (#2) and purple 4 (#1)	6
Purple 3 (#2) and white	2
Purple 4 (#1) and gray 3 (#5)	6
Purple 4 (#1) and white	4
Purple 4 (#1) and green (#8)	2
Gray 3 (#5) and gray 2 (#6)	6
Gray 3 (#5) and white	2
Gray 2 (#6) and gray 1 (#7)	6
Gray 2 (#6) and white	2
Gray 1 (#7) and green (#8)	6
Gray 1 (#7) and white	8
Green (#8) and white	6
White and white	2

TIP

Stack up blocks that are the same and organize them according to the chart. This will help you stay organized when you start assembling rows.

Quilt Assembly

Refer to the quilt photos (pages 94 and 95) and to the quilt assembly diagrams, at right.

1. Sew together the blocks into rows, matching the seams. Press the seams open.

2. Sew together the rows, matching the seams. Press the seams open.

Backing

For the crib size:

Trim the backing to approximately 44″ × 54″, piecing as needed.

For the twin size:

1. Iron the 3 pieces of fabric listed in the dye chart for the backing.

2. Trim off the selvages and square up the ends of each piece of fabric so you have clean lines for piecing.

3. In the order of your choosing, sew together the 3 pieces along the long edges to make 1 large piece. Press the seams open.

4. Trim to 70″ × 86″.

FINISHING

Refer to Quiltmaking Basics: Finishing (page 130) to layer, quilt, and bind the quilt, using the remaining fabric pieces for the binding.

Quilt assembly diagrams

Crib-size *Knit Quilt* in purple with green

QUILTED SHIBORI WALLHANGING

FINISHED QUILT: 40″ × 40″

Shibori is the traditional Japanese method of resist dyeing fabric to create patterns. Resist dyeing means that areas of the fabric are blocked so they won't accept dye. You are probably familiar with tie-dye. Shibori is tie-dye's much cooler older cousin. There are many different shibori techniques, but my favorite is itajime, or clamped resist. This method creates bold, graphic patterns that are often symmetrical. I love to use clamped shibori in quilts because I find a lot of similarity to traditional quilt patterns in the symmetrical patterns created by the itajime.

MATERIALS AND EQUIPMENT

Yardage is based on 44″-wide fabric.

- 1¼ yards undyed white fabric for the top

- Hanging sleeve: ¼ yard

- Binding: ½ yard (This would be a great place to use up scraps from other dye projects. You will need about 200 linear inches of 2½″-wide strips to bind the quilt.)

- Backing: 44″ × 44″ (This a good place to experiment with one of your own dye recipes.)

- Batting: 44″ × 44″

- 2 pieces of wood that are the same size (I used 2″ × 4″ pieces.)

- 2 standard (2″) spring clamps

- Bucket: large plastic tub, such as the container that stores your dyes and auxiliaries (page 14)

DYEING INSTRUCTIONS

1. Mix up your dye solution. For this piece, I dissolved 1 tablespoon New Black dye powder in 1 cup warm water. Feel free to experiment and make your own color. Darker colors will make the quilt much more bold and modern feeling, so use at least 1 tablespoon dye in 1 cup water. Set the dye solution aside.

2. Fold your fabric into a bundle following the illustrations. It is important to thoroughly press each fold in order to get crisp resisted areas.

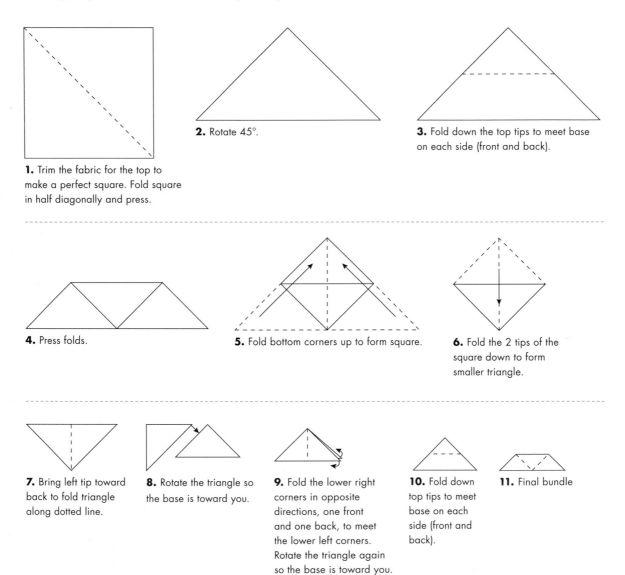

1. Trim the fabric for the top to make a perfect square. Fold square in half diagonally and press.

2. Rotate 45°.

3. Fold down the top tips to meet base on each side (front and back).

4. Press folds.

5. Fold bottom corners up to form square.

6. Fold the 2 tips of the square down to form smaller triangle.

7. Bring left tip toward back to fold triangle along dotted line.

8. Rotate the triangle so the base is toward you.

9. Fold the lower right corners in opposite directions, one front and one back, to meet the lower left corners. Rotate the triangle again so the base is toward you.

10. Fold down top tips to meet base on each side (front and back).

11. Final bundle

3. Make a sandwich with 2 pieces of wood the same size on either side of the fabric bundle.

4. Place a clamp on the top folds of the triangle bundle and on the base of the triangle so the wood pieces are held together tightly.

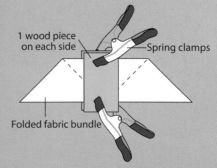

1 wood piece on each side — Spring clamps

Folded fabric bundle

Clamp wood on both sides of folded fabric.

5. Wet the bundle. Squeeze out excess water and place it in the plastic tub.

6. Add 2 teaspoons soda ash to the dye solution and stir thoroughly.

7. Pour the dye solution over the bundle and let it sit for 30 minutes. During the 30 minutes, squeeze the bundle a few times with gloved hands and turn it over occasionally so the dye can seep in evenly.

8. After 30 minutes, unclamp the bundle and wash out the fabric (page 23).

9. Dry and iron the dyed fabric.

10. To finish the piece, trim to square up the fabric piece.

FINISHING

1. Refer to Quiltmaking Basics: Finishing (page 130) to layer, quilt, and bind the quilt.

2. Make and sew on a hanging sleeve (page 134).

Quilted Shibori Wallhanging

PIECED BLUE AND BLACK SHIBORI QUILT

Pieced shibori quilts are fast and fun to make, and they look impressive. Try different folding and clamping methods and try using one or more colors of dye solution poured on different parts of the clamped bundles. Make sketches of how you fold the fabric and keep notes on what dye colors you used, and before long you will have a great collection of your own hand-dyed itajime shibori fabric and a wealth of knowledge for making more.

I think shibori fabric looks best in combination with solid fabrics that coordinate. To me, a quilt made entirely of different shibori fabrics pieced together appears quite busy, and I think the solid fabrics accentuate the patterning in the shibori.

The proportion of shibori to solid fabric is up to you. My version of this quilt is a little over half shibori and a little under half blue and black. Use your own favorite colors and the instructions below to create your own stunning shibori crib-size quilt. Then draw on your creativity to make a shibori quilt in any size.

MATERIALS AND EQUIPMENT

Yardage is based on 44″-wide fabric.

- 1½ yards undyed white for the top

- Binding: ½ yard undyed white

- Backing: 1⅝ yards undyed white

- Batting: 44″ × 54″

- Buckets: 2 gallon-size containers for 2 solid colors, a shallow plastic container for the shibori piece, 1 gallon-size container for binding, and a 2- or 3-gallon container for backing

- 2 pieces of wood that are the same size (I used 2″ × 4″.)

- 1 or 2 standard (2″) spring clamps

DYEING INSTRUCTIONS

Refer to How to Dye Fabric (page 20) as needed.

1. Fold and clamp the piece of fabric you cut for the shibori piece, following the steps in the illustrations. Press the folds with an iron and make sure the clamp is very secure.

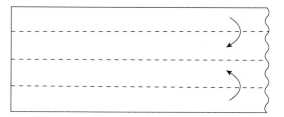

A. Fold the fabric in half, press with an iron, and then open the fold. Then fold the edges of the fabric toward the center crease.

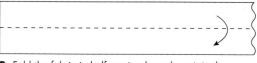

B. Fold the fabric in half again along the original crease, enclosing the edges from the previous step.

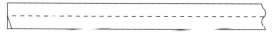

C. Rotate the fabric so that the open side is on top. Then fold the front flap down so the top edge meets the bottom edge. The fabric should be a quarter of the original height.

D. Fold the bottom left corner up, into half an isosceles triangle.

E. Turn the fabric over and then fold the lower corner up to form a full isosceles triangle. Accordion fold the fabric, following the previous isosceles folds, until you end up with a triangle fabric bundle.

F. Make a fabric sandwich with a piece of wood on either side of the bundle and clamp it all together with a spring clamp. If the bundle is too big, use 2 clamps.

2. Mix a soda ash solution of 1 gallon warm water plus ½ cup soda ash. Stir the mixture thoroughly to dissolve the soda ash, and always wear gloves when working with soda ash. This solution is often called a "soda soak."

3. Soak the folded and clamped bundle in the soda soak for 10 minutes.

TIP

> Soaking the fabric in this soda ash solution (soda soak) is different from the dyeing process used for the other projects in the book, but it is a common way to get the soda ash into the dyeing process. When soaking fabric in a soda soak prior to dyeing, you do not need to add soda ash again later in the process.

4. While the fabric is soaking, make the dye solution. For pieced shibori quilts, I make 1 cup of dye solution for each color that I will be using. For my dye solutions, I use 3 teaspoons of dye powder in 1 cup of warm water for dark, bold colors. If you prefer paler colors, use less dye. For the pictured quilt (page 111), I made 1 solution using Cerulean Blue and 1 solution using New Black.

5. With gloved hands, remove the fabric bundle from the soda ash solution and gently squeeze out some of the solution. Place the fabric in the shallow plastic container. Pour some of each color over exposed parts of the bundle and make sure the dye solution gets into the folds of the fabric. You won't be using all the dye solution, just a small amount of each color. Let the fabric sit for about 30 minutes.

6. While the shibori fabric is sitting, dye the other pieces of fabric. At this point, there is a lot of dye solution left. You still have the fabric for the blue and the fabric for the black to dye. You can use as much or as little as you want of the dye solution to dye these pieces of fabric, depending on how dark you want the color to be. If you use all the dye solution, your fabric will be dark. If you use only a little, the color will be pale. Any dye solution that is left over can be kept and reused later or used for the binding and backing fabric. Dye dissolved in water will last for about a day, covered and stored at room temperature.

Refer to How Much Dye to Use (page 139) for the amounts of water, salt, and soda ash to use on the 2 remaining pieces of cloth. Follow the procedure for solid-color dyeing in How to Dye Fabric (page 20), using the dye solution instead of dry dye powder.

7. Wash out all the fabric (page 23).

8. Dry and iron the dyed fabric.

CONSTRUCTION

1. For the quilt top, trim the fabrics to size so that they are perfect rectangles and allow for a ¼˝ seam allowance. Trim the shibori to 20½˝ × 50½˝, the blue to 5½˝ × 50½˝, and the black to 15½˝ × 50½˝.

2. Sew the pieces together and press the seams.

FINISHING

1. Trim the backing fabric to 44˝ × 54˝.

2. Refer to Quiltmaking Basics: Finishing (page 130) to layer, quilt, and bind the quilt.

3. Make and sew on a hanging sleeve (page 134) if desired.

Pieced Blue and Black Shibori Quilt

STRIPED
LANDSCAPE QUILT

FINISHED QUILT: 60″ × 60″

I have been working on a series of landscape quilts since 2010. I love being outside—hiking, gardening, picking apples, and hanging out around a campfire are some of my favorite activities. As I've gotten older, I've found that I don't have as much time to spend outside as I would like, so I started creating these quilts based on the weather, quality of light, and land around me. The goal of these quilts is to capture an abstracted view of the sky or landscape during especially beautiful or dramatic moments.

You can make your own abstracted landscape quilts by paying close attention to your environment. If you don't do it already, start going outside and looking up at the sky regularly. Pay attention to shadows and how the trees and grass look at different times of day. Or, if you live in the city, look at how the buildings change color as the sun travels across the sky. Carry a camera with you, or use the camera on your phone, to capture the moments that speak to you. I do this whenever

I can and use the photographs as inspiration for these quilts.

When you have chosen a photograph that you want to use for a quilt design, analyze it closely for the most important colors and the proportions of those colors. For example, you may have just a tiny hint of bright blue in a field of dark clouds. Look for gradations within your photographs. The dark clouds may be a gradation from gray to purple. In your quilt, you will try to create the same proportion of color—a lot of dark grays or purples with just a small hint of bright blue—by adjusting the size of your strips of fabric accordingly. It is the proportion of color and the range of values that make a quilt work.

Making these quilts is a great way to become more comfortable with mixing custom colors, figuring out how much dye you need to mix, and creating your own gradations. Try making one of your own landscape quilts based on your photograph and my instructions that follow.

DANGER
HIGH VOLTAGE
KEEP AWAY

MATERIALS AND EQUIPMENT

Yardage is based on 44˝-wide fabric.

- 6 yards undyed white fabric for the top

- 4½ yards for the backing and binding

- Batting: 66˝ × 66˝

- Buckets: 1 quart-size container for each color or gradation in the quilt, 1 gallon-size container for the binding, and a 2- or 3-gallon container for the backing

FABRIC PREPARATION

1. Decide how many colors you want in your quilt, including the gradation steps. For example, in *Iowa in May* (page 117) I used 16 colors. *Kansas in August* (page 117) has 3 different gradations: a 6-step monochromatic purple gradation, a 5-step monochromatic yellow gradation, and a 5-step gradation adding black to the yellow.

TIP

I find it helpful to draw my quilts to scale on graph paper. You can figure out the color order and numbers of gradation steps this way using colored pencils or markers, and it will serve as your map later for piecing.

2. Divide the length of the quilt by the number of colors from Step 1 to find out how wide the strips will be. In *Kansas in August*, this would be 60˝ (the length of the quilt) divided by 16 colors = 3.75˝. For your first try, it is easiest to make the strips all the same width. As you get more comfortable, you can adjust the strip size depending on how much of each color you want.

3. Add 2˝ to this number to allow for shrinkage, trimming, and seam allowances. In our example, the width of the strips I need to cut is 3.75˝ + 2˝ = 5.75˝.

4. Cut a strip for each of your colors, the width you calculated by the width of the quilt + 5˝, again to allow for shrinkage and trimming. In our example, I would cut 16 strips that are 5.75˝ × 65˝. To do this, start by cutting or tearing a length of fabric to 65˝. Then cut or tear the 5.75˝ strips from this fabric.

DYEING INSTRUCTIONS

1. It is helpful to figure out the square footage of your fabric strips so you have a starting point for your dye recipes. Using the same example of *Kansas in August*, the strips are 5.75″ × 65″. To find the square feet, multiply the width by length and then divide by 144. Our example is 5.75″ × 65″ = 373.75 square inches divided by 144 = 2.6 square feet. You can compare this measurement to the amounts in this chart for general square footage of ⅛ yard, ¼ yard, ½ yard, or full yard of fabric to figure out how much water, salt, dye, and soda ash to use.

	⅛ YARD	¼ YARD	½ YARD	1 YARD
SQUARE FEET	1.25	2.5	5.5	11

My example of 2.6 square feet is closest to ¼ yard of 44″-wide fabric, so I would use the quantities of water, salt, soda ash, and dye for ¼ yard of fabric from the chart How Much Dye to Use (page 139) for each of my 16 dye baths.

2. If each of the colors is completely different, set up each dye bath individually and measure out different colors and amounts of dye for each of the strips of fabric.

3. If, however, you have one or more gradations in your quilt design, you need to figure out quantities of dye for each gradation. First, decide what the value of the darkest color is. For a very dark value, you will use double the amount of dye listed for dark colors in the chart How Much Dye to Use (page 139). For a medium value, you will use the amount of dye listed for dark colors.

For example: The purple gradation in *Kansas in August* starts with a very dark purple. From the chart How Much Dye to Use (page 139), a dark value on ¼ yard of fabric requires ½ teaspoon of dye. For the very dark purple color, double the quantity of dye to 1 teaspoon. This can be mixed from different dye colors to make 1 teaspoon.

4. Dissolve the dye powder in ¼ cup warm water. Stir it well to thoroughly dissolve the dye. This is the dye solution.

5. Put the fabric strips needed for the gradation in a container of warm water to soak while you set up the number of dye baths you need for the gradation. You can refer to the gradation processes in *Circle Quilt* (page 62), *Pineapple Log Cabin Quilt* (page 79), or *Knit Quilt* (page 90), or use the general gradation process below.

- For ¼-yard pieces of fabric, each dye bath container starts with 2 cups water and ½ tablespoon salt. (You will need to adjust as needed for larger pieces of fabric.)

- Repeat the following for as many gradations as you want to make. The more steps you have, the lighter the color will be at the end of the gradation:

> Add ⅛ cup (or 2 tablespoons) dye solution to dye bath #1 and stir it well.

> Add ⅛ cup water to the dye solution and stir well.

Continue with this until each of your dye baths has dye solution added. Discard the last ⅛ cup of dye solution.

6. Add a piece of wet fabric to each dye bath and stir all the dye baths well for about 10 minutes.

7. Add the required amount of soda ash from the chart How Much Dye to Use (page 139) to each dye bath and stir well. Then stir as much as you want for 30 minutes, depending on how mottled or how solid you want the fabric to be.

8. Wash out the fabric (page 23).

9. Dry and iron the strips of fabric.

10. Repeat the steps as needed for other color gradations in your quilt design, if you have them. Or dye individual colors until all the fabric strips are dyed.

11. Dye the binding and backing fabric to coordinate with the quilt top. You will have to piece the back, so think about how to play with the piecing and the colors to make the back its own composition.

CONSTRUCTION

1. For the top, trim each strip of fabric to the width you calculated earlier, plus ½″ for seam allowances.

TIP

> Arrange the strips in order on the floor or on a table. If you love how the arrangement looks, keep going. If you're not too excited about it at this point, don't be afraid to change things up. Sometimes colors look a lot different after they're dyed, and you might decide to change the order of the strips. That's okay! You might also decide that you need a few more colors inserted in the quilt. Keep dyeing strips of fabric and inserting them into the quilt until you are pleased with the overall effect.

2. Sew the pieces together in the order you decided, using a ¼″ seam allowance.

3. Press the seams to one side or open. (You get to decide!)

FINISHING

1. Piece the backing as planned and trim to 66″ × 66″.

2. Refer to Quiltmaking Basics: Finishing (page 130) to layer, quilt, and bind the quilt.

Kansas in August

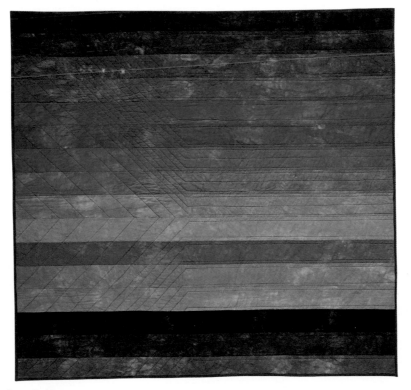

Iowa in May

GALLERY

Skyscape Quilt in Blue and Rust, 40˝ × 50˝

This is one of my favorite quilts. It was one of the first landscape quilts I made using gradations. From the top of the quilt it is a series of four gradations: from dark blue to maroon, then a maroon monochromatic gradation, then light maroon to turquoise, and then dark brown to rust. The light maroon to turquoise gradation is flipped around to make the single strip of light turquoise stand out more.

Iowa in July, 40" × 50"

This quilt was inspired by the sky just after an evening thunderstorm in Iowa. The sky was still dark with clouds, but the clouds were starting to part, allowing the setting sun to cast a bright swath of light across the wet fields of corn. I dyed the green fabric in a six-step gradation, starting with the brightest green and gradually adding black to subsequent dye baths. For this quilt, I played with the proportion of color by making the yellow and orange of the sunset the skinniest strips. The sky colors are light and dark versions of blue and gray.

One type of gradation is the shade gradation—adding black to a color. This quilt is a shade gradation on a three-color gradation. I started with orange, yellow, and turquoise, and then mixed the yellow and orange in equal proportions and the yellow and turquoise in equal proportions to get the green and yellowish-orange colors. After those five colors were mixed, I made a six-step shade gradation of each color, so that moving down the quilt, more and more black was added to the dye baths until they all look nearly identical in the bottom row. After piecing the top, I folded and clamped it and immersed it in thiox, just as in the *Rainbow Shibori* quilt (page 126).

Paint Chip Shibori, 40" × 50"

CMYK Quilt, 40˝ × 50˝

My background is in printmaking, and that is where I first learned the magic of color mixing. CMYK are the process colors: cyan, magenta, yellow, and key (or black), and in some print-making methods, the four colors are layered to create multicolored prints. As a tribute to my printmaking past, I created this CMYK color block quilt. The extra-nerdy color-mixing element to this quilt is that unlike CMYK inks in printmaking, each color in this quilt was custom mixed by me. In other words, I didn't simply use magenta or cyan dye; I mixed them from at least three other dye colors. After I mixed my own CMYK colors, each one was used in a five-step monochromatic gradation.

My husband and I bought our first house a few years ago, and when we moved in, all the walls were painted a sort of neutral beige color. I immediately started collecting paint chips from the hardware store in an attempt to choose colors for each room. After three years, most of the house is still neutral beige, but I have drawers full of paint chips. My paint chip collection inspired this quilt and another orange version. You can think of this quilt in two ways. It is either five rows of five-step monochromatic gradations or five columns of five-step shade gradations. In reality, it is both—25 colors made by mixing varying quantities of blue and black.

Blue Color Block Quilt, 40˝ × 50˝

Iowa in Summer, 40" × 50"

I firmly believe in being flexible and changing plans when something doesn't work out. With hand-dyed fabric, it is easy to let things get too precious. I get it. Dyeing fabric takes a lot of time. It's hard to spend a whole day or several days dyeing fabric, then another couple of days piecing a top, and then decide it's no good. But that is exactly what happened with this quilt. It started out as a twin-size quilt with something like 40 different colors in several gradations. Once all the fabric was dyed and the top was pieced, I stepped back and thought, "That is one boring quilt." After a couple more days trying to convince myself it wasn't boring, I finally realized the only thing to do was to cut it all apart and make it into two smaller quilts. This is one of the two quilts that emerged from the mess. In the end, I am so glad it happened this way because it made me think about perspective and different compositional elements and led to a body of work that I might not have made otherwise.

Rainbow Shibori, 86″ × 96″

In my head, this quilt looked very different. I approached it as a very simple series of gradations: from black to red, red to yellow, and yellow to black. Of course, as we know, black should be thought of as dark gray-blue when dyeing fabric (page 26). So of course a gradation from blue to red, red to yellow, and yellow to blue would result in a rainbow. Even though the quilt is not at all what I expected, I am happy with the results. I dyed one piece of each gradation step as a dark value and light value. When piecing the quilt, I cut the dark piece of each color in half to create a column of lighter color in the middle of the quilt. After piecing, I folded and clamped the quilt top and immersed it in thiourea dioxide, or thiox—a chemical that removes dye from fabric. A substitute for thiox is Rit Color Remover. Removing dyed color is called discharging.

Iowa in January, 40″ × 50″

This quilt was not based on a real day, but rather a collection of memories of what bright winter days in Iowa look like. Sometimes the air is so crisp and clean and the sky is so blue that I feel like I can touch it. At the horizon the sky is almost white, and it deepens as you look up. The light cerulean fabric for this quilt was dyed as one piece of fabric, and then I cut it apart in various widths to be interspersed with a five-step blue-gray gradation. I'm not sure why I chose to use purple in this quilt, but the vision I had in my mind of this quilt included a strip of reddish purple, so I had to include it.

There is a strange kind of light that sometimes happens in Kansas before thunderstorms. The sky begins to darken and turn purple, but the sun is still shining and making the fields glow. Everything turns the same value, and there is an eerie look to the light. This quilt is an attempt at capturing that effect. The fields are a five-step gradation from light yellow to greenish brown. The fabric was dyed in half-yard pieces and then cut into strips for improvisational piecing. The top section is two very close values of purple/gray and one piece of monochromatic mottled purple fabric. As with *Iowa in Summer* (page 125), this quilt plays with perspective. It's hard to tell whether we are above the fields looking down or looking across the horizon at the fields.

Kansas Fields, 40″ × 50″

QUILTMAKING BASICS:
Finishing

MAKING A QUILT SANDWICH

Once your quilt top is sewn together and all the seams are pressed according to the directions, you are ready to assemble the quilt sandwich: the pieced top, the quilt batting, and the back. For some quilts, the back might also be pieced, and this must be done before assembling the sandwich. Before you start, make sure your quilt top and the back are all pressed smooth and that the backing and batting are each at least 2˝ larger than the quilt top on each side.

Layering

1. Place the quilt back on a table, or on the floor if it is a large quilt, wrong side up. The back should be gently and evenly smoothed and stretched so that it is taut against the floor, but not pulled so tightly that you warp the grain of the fabric. A quilt back that is not gently stretched out is more likely to cause small puckers and creases as you start to quilt. Start in the middle of the top side and tape the quilt back to the floor with a piece of blue painter's tape or masking tape. Go to the bottom side, gently pull the fabric toward you, and tape down the middle of the bottom edge. Repeat with the left and then right sides. After the sides are taped, follow the same procedure with the corners. Depending on the size of the quilt, you may need to add more pieces of tape between the corner and middle pieces. If you are working on carpet, use T-pins instead of tape.

2. After the back is taped down, gently center the quilt batting over the backing fabric. Start in the middle of the batting and gently smooth it out with your hands so there are no bumps or wrinkles.

3. Gently lay the quilt top, right side up, centered over the batting. Again, start in the center and gently smooth the quilt top out over the batting. Make sure there is batting and backing sticking out all 4 sides of the quilt top. The extra batting and backing are there in case your quilt top stretches or shifts a little during the quilting process. The edges will be trimmed after the quilting is completed.

Basting

Basting holds the quilt sandwich together while you are quilting. Thorough basting also prevents the layers from shifting. Use curved safety pins, sometimes called quilter's basting pins. For a large quilt, you will need about 300 safety pins. Start in the center and work your way out toward the edges, pinning every 3˝–4˝. Make sure the pins go through all 3 layers. I usually divide my quilt into quadrants by pinning horizontally through the middle of the quilt, then vertically, and then filling in each quadrant with a grid of pins.

After the entire quilt has been basted with safety pins, you can remove the tape from the quilt back. This is also when I prefer to step back and decide what my quilting plan is going to be and mark any quilting designs that need to be marked with chalk.

QUILTING

Quilting, whether by hand or machine, enhances the pieced design of the quilt. You may choose to quilt in-the-ditch, echo the pieced blocks, use patterns from quilting design books and stencils, or do your own free-motion quilting. I generally prefer to quilt using only straight lines, with as few stops and starts in the middle of the quilt as possible. I find that quilting ¼″–½″ from each seam gives the blocks a lot of dimension without being distracting. Think about the color of thread you're using and whether you want it to blend with the quilt top or stand out as another design element. I like to use a couple of different colors of thread on a quilt to highlight certain areas and add visual interest. Remember to check your batting manufacturer's recommendations for how close the quilting lines must be.

BINDING

Trim excess batting and backing from the quilt even with the edges of the quilt top. Make sure your quilt is squared up; trim again if necessary.

Double-Fold Straight-Grain Binding

PREPARING THE BINDING

1. Cut the binding strips 2½″ wide and piece them together with diagonal seams to make a continuous binding strip. Trim the seam allowance to ¼″. Press the seams open.

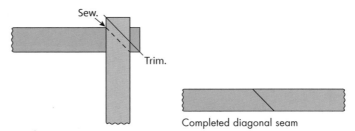

Sew.

Trim.

Sew from corner to corner.

Completed diagonal seam

2. Press the entire strip in half lengthwise with wrong sides together.

SEWING THE BINDING TO THE QUILT

1. With raw edges even, pin the binding to the edge of the quilt near the middle of a side, leaving the first few inches of the binding unattached. For binding that will be finished by hand sewing, you will sew the

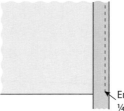

End stitching ¼″ from corner.

Stitch to ¼″ from corner.

binding to the front of the quilt. I sometimes prefer to completely machine sew my binding and will pin and sew the binding to the back of the quilt. Start sewing, using a ¼″ seam allowance. Stop ¼″ away from the first corner and backstitch.

2. Lift the presser foot and needle. Rotate the quilt a quarter turn. Fold the binding at a right angle so it extends straight above the quilt and the fold forms a 45° angle in the corner.

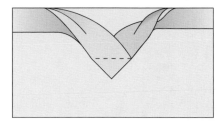

First fold for miter

3. Then bring the binding strip down even with the edge of the quilt. Begin sewing at the folded edge. Repeat in the same manner at all the corners.

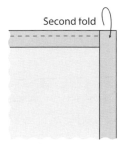

Second fold alignment

4. Continue stitching until you are about 10″–12″ from the beginning of the binding strip. Place the 2 ends of the binding smoothly along the edge of the quilt and trim them so they overlap by 2½″.

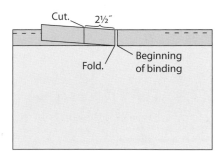

5. Open up the 2 ends and place them right sides together and perpendicular to each other. Overlap the ends by about ¼″ and pin them together. Stitch diagonally across the ends and trim the seam allowance to ¼″. Press the seam open.

6. Refold the binding back in half and realign with the edge of the quilt. Pin in place and stitch the binding to the quilt.

7. Press the binding toward the raw edge and then fold the binding to the back of the quilt for hand finishing the binding, or to the front of the quilt for machine finishing the binding. If you want to hang your quilt, this is the time to add a sleeve on the back. Refer to Making a Hanging Sleeve for a Quilt (page 134). Pin or clip the binding in place. To hand sew, use a blind stitch and miter the corners as you come to them. To machine sew, topstitch close to the edge of the binding, using a walking foot and thread that matches the binding. Miter the corners as you come to them.

MAKING A HANGING SLEEVE FOR A QUILT

The best way to hang a quilt is to sew a sleeve on the back and insert a wooden slat with screw eyes through the sleeve. A sleeve should be made before the binding is added, if possible. However, it can be added after the binding.

1. Cut a piece of fabric the width of the quilt × 8″. Press the short ends under ¼″, then another ¼″ to create a clean edge. Sew the folded ends in place.

2. Fold the sleeve in half lengthwise with wrong sides together and stitch the raw edges, using a scant ¼″ seam allowance and back-stitching at both ends.

3. If you are adding this sleeve *after* the binding, skip to Step 4. If you are adding this sleeve *before* the binding, align the raw edge of the tube with the top edge of the quilt. Pin in place. Stitch the binding to the quilt, stitching the sleeve in place with the binding across the top of the quilt, and complete the binding as you normally do. Blind stitch the bottom edge of the sleeve to the quilt, going through the quilt batting but not all the way through to the quilt top.

4. If this sleeve is being added *after* the binding, press the sleeve flat, with the seam pressed open and centered as shown. Align the tube at the top of the quilt, just below the binding, with the open seam against the quilt. Blind stitch the top and bottom edges of the sleeve to the quilt, going through the quilt batting but not all the way through to the quilt top.

5. You're almost done! At this point I almost always run my quilts through a wash and dry cycle to fluff them up and give them some texture.

Making the Wooden Slat

1. Cut a ½″ × 1½″ wooden slat the width of the sleeve. The overall length of the wooden slat, including the screw eyes (which you add in the next step), should be just shorter than the width of the quilt, so the slat won't show when the quilt is hanging. Sand the edges smooth if necessary.

2. Insert a screw eye into each end of the slat, about ½″ down from the top of the slat.

3. Insert the slat into the sleeve and hang the quilt on the wall, using the screw eyes to nail through.

HELPFUL INFORMATION

Modern Color—An Illustrated Guide to Dyeing Fabric for Modern Quilts

DYE RECIPE CARDS

I find it helpful to keep careful notes on how I mix my colors so that I can easily re-create them. Filling out a recipe card before you start dyeing is a great idea because it will help you remember what you're doing as you start dyeing your fabric. It is also easy to forget what colors you used and how much of each one, so if you fill out a card before you start, you don't have to worry about remembering later. I write both my dye quantities and the proportion of color I used, in case I want to make the color lighter or darker in the future. Cut a corner off your fabric after it has been dyed and washed and staple it to the card for reference.

Here are two examples of how I might fill out a card, with notes to help myself remember what worked and what didn't.

COLOR NAME: Medium Teal

FABRIC TYPE AND AMOUNT	Kona Cotton White PFD, 2 yards
DYE PROPORTION	1/2 Cerulean Blue, 1/4 New Black, 1/4 Lemon Yellow
DYE AMOUNT	2 tsp.* Cerulean Blue, 1 tsp. New Black, 1 tsp. Lemon Yellow
WATER	4 quarts
SALT	1/4 cup
SODA ASH	4 tsp.
NOTES	Stirred regularly to make even. Next time use more Lemon Yellow and less black.

tsp. = teaspoon

COLOR NAME: Light Mottled Orange

FABRIC TYPE AND AMOUNT	Natural muslin, 1/2 yard
DYE PROPORTION	Equal parts Sun Yellow, Deep Yellow, Light Red
DYE AMOUNT	1/16 tsp.* Sun Yellow, 1/16 tsp. Deep Yellow, 1/16 tsp. Light Red
WATER	1 quart
SALT	No
SODA ASH	1 tsp. dissolved in 2 Tbsp.* water
NOTES	Dissolved each dye color separately in 1/4 cup water. Poured on in sections. Minimal squeezing. Good color.

tsp. = teaspoon; Tbsp. = tablespoon

COLOR NAME:

FABRIC TYPE AND AMOUNT	
DYE PROPORTION	
DYE AMOUNT	
WATER	
SALT	
SODA ASH	
NOTES	

COLOR NAME:

FABRIC TYPE AND AMOUNT	
DYE PROPORTION	
DYE AMOUNT	
WATER	
SALT	
SODA ASH	
NOTES	

COLOR NAME:

FABRIC TYPE AND AMOUNT	
DYE PROPORTION	
DYE AMOUNT	
WATER	
SALT	
SODA ASH	
NOTES	

HOW MUCH DYE TO USE

SMOOTH, EVEN COLOR

	¼ YARD FABRIC	½ YARD FABRIC	1 YARD FABRIC
DYE POWDER, PALE	1/16–⅛ tsp.*	⅛–¼ tsp.	¼–½ tsp.
DYE POWDER, MEDIUM	¼ tsp.	½ tsp.	1–2 tsp.
DYE POWDER, DARK	¾ tsp.	2 tsp.	3–4 tsp.
WATER	2 cups	1 quart	2 quarts
SALT	½ Tbsp.*	1 Tbsp.	2 Tbsp.
SODA ASH	½ tsp.	1 tsp.	2 tsp.
WATER SOFTENER (if needed)	⅛ tsp.	¼ tsp.	½ tsp.

tsp. = teaspoon; Tbsp. = tablespoon

MOTTLED COLOR

	¼ YARD FABRIC	½ YARD FABRIC	1 YARD FABRIC
DYE POWDER, PALE	1/32–1/16 tsp.*	1/16–⅛ tsp.	⅛–¼ tsp.
DYE POWDER, MEDIUM	⅛ tsp.	¼ tsp.	½–1 tsp.
DYE POWDER, DARK	¼ tsp.	½ tsp.	1–2 tsp.
WATER**	½ cup	1 cup	2 cups
SODA ASH	¼ tsp.	½ tsp.	1 tsp.
WATER SOFTENER (if needed)	⅛ tsp.	¼ tsp.	½ tsp.

tsp. = teaspoon

*** Combine the dye powder with the listed amount of water and pour over the damp fabric.*

USEFUL CONVERSIONS

3 tsp. = 1 Tbsp. = ½ oz.
6 tsp. = 2 Tbsp. = ⅛ cup = 1 oz.
4 Tbsp. = ¼ cup = 2 oz.
16 Tbsp. = 1 cup = 8 oz.
4 cups = 1 quart = 32 oz.
4 quarts = 1 gallon = 128 oz.

RESOURCES

DYE SUPPLIES

DHARMA TRADING COMPANY

Dye, fabric for dyeing, auxiliaries

dharmatrading.com

800-542-5227

PRO CHEMICAL & DYE

Dye and auxiliaries

prochemicalanddye.com

800-228-9393 orders;

508-676-3838 free technical support

JACQUARD DYES AND AUXILIARIES ARE AVAILABLE FROM ART SUPPLY STORES.

QUILTING SUPPLIES

Check your local quilt, fabric, or craft shop for basic quilting supplies. If you can't find what you are looking for in the store or online, check the following manufacturers' websites for information on where to find their products.

BERNINA USA

Sewing machines

berninausa.com

CONNECTING THREADS

Cotton quilting thread

connectingthreads.com

DRITZ

Pins, needles, curved safety pins, marking tools

dritz.com/brands/dritz

GINGHER

Scissors, rotary cutters, shears

gingher.com

ROBERT KAUFMAN

Kona Cotton PFD

robertkaufman.com

OLFA

Rotary cutters, rotary cutting mats

olfa.com

OMNIGRID

Rotary cutting rulers, rotary cutting mats

dritz.com/brands/omnigrid

THE WARM COMPANY

Quilt batting

warmcompany.com

WEST ELM

Down and down–alternative pillow inserts with 100% cotton shells

westelm.com

RECOMMENDED READING

Albers, Josef. *Interaction of Color: Revised and Expanded Edition.* New Haven, CT, and London: Yale University Press, 2006.

Holstein, Jonathan. *Abstract Design in American Quilts: A Biography of an Exhibition.* Louisville, KY: Kentucky Quilt Project, 1991.

Proctor, Richard M. *Principles of Pattern Design.* New York: Van Nostrand Reinhold, 1969.

Smucker, Janneken, Patricia Cox Crews, and Linda Welters. *Amish Crib Quilts from the Midwest: The Sara Miller Collection.* Intercourse, PA: Good Books, 2003.

Stoddard, Patricia Ormsby. *Ralli Quilts: Traditional Textiles from Pakistan and India.* Atglen, PA: Schiffer Publishing, 2003.

Wada, Yoshiko Iwamoto, Mary Kellogg Rice, and Jane Barton. *Shibori: The Inventive Art of Japanese Shaped Resist Dyeing.* Tokyo: Kodansha America, 1983.

Basic Quiltmaking Books

Bonner, Natalia. *Beginner's Guide to Free-Motion Quilting.* Concord, CA: C&T Publishing, 2012.

Hartman, Elizabeth. *The Practical Guide to Patchwork.* Concord, CA: C&T Publishing, 2010.

Pease, Bethany. *Modern Quilting Designs.* Concord, CA: C&T Publishing, 2012.

ABOUT THE AUTHOR

Photo by Rita Clark

KIM EICHLER-MESSMER grew up in Iowa. She learned how to sew in fifth grade, when she made a quilt out of old shirts with her father. She went on to study engineering, Spanish, Portuguese, drawing, and printmaking before taking a textiles class in 2000. Kim received an MFA in textiles from the University of Kansas in 2007. She was an Artist in Residence at Arrowmont School of Arts and Crafts in Gatlinburg, Tennessee. Her work has been exhibited nationally in numerous group and solo shows. Her quilts have also been featured in West Elm, Apartment Therapy, and Design Sponge. Kim currently lives in Kansas City, where she does math daily, grows tomatoes, hugs cats, and is an assistant professor in the Fiber Department of the Kansas City Art Institute.